# Narrative Strategies in Canadian Literature

# Narrative Strategies in Canadian Literature

Feminism and Postcolonialism

**Edited by**
**Coral Ann Howells and Lynette Hunter**

Open University Press
Milton Keynes · Philadelphia

Open University Press
Celtic Court
22 Ballmoor
Buckingham
MK18 1XW

and
1900 Frost Road, Suite 101
Bristol, PA 19007, US

First published 1991

*British Library Cataloguing in Publication Data*

Narrative strategies in Canadian literature:
Feminism and postcolonialism.
  I. Howells, Coral A.  II. Hunter, Lynette
  810.9000971

  ISBN 0-335-09770-7

*Library of Congress Cataloging in Publication Number Available*

Typeset by Colset Private Limited, Singapore
Printed and bound in Great Britain by St Edmundsbury Press Ltd
Bury St Edmunds, Suffolk

# Contents

# List of Contributors

*Shirley Chew* teaches English literature at the University of Leeds. She is the editor of *Arthur Hugh Clough: Selected Poems* and *Re-visions of Canadian Literature*. She has published on English and on Commonwealth writers in various journals, and is at present collaborating on a critical volume on recent literature from Commonwealth countries.

*Peter Easingwood* is a Lecturer in English at the University of Dundee, where he has also served as Director of American Studies. He has co-edited two collections of essays on Canadian literature and culture and has contributed another essay on Margaret Laurence to a recent collection published by the Macmillan Press.

*Andrew Gurr* has taught at the universities of Wellington, Auckland, Canterbury (New Zealand), Cambridge, Leeds, Reading (UK), Nairobi (Kenya), UCLA, Folger Shakespeare Library (USA). He is the author of books on Shakespeare and Elizabethan theatre, Katherine Mansfield and other Commonwealth literature, and is editor of *Journal of Commonwealth Literature* and *Modern Language Review*.

*Coral Ann Howells*, an Australian who has lived in England for over 25 years, is Reader in Canadian Literature at the University of Reading. Her publications include *Private and Fictional Worlds: Canadian Women Novelists of the 1970s and 80s*, and *Jean Rhys*.

*Lynette Hunter*, a Canadian who has lived in England for nearly 20 years, teaches Canadian Literature in the School of English at the University of Leeds. She has written a number of books on twentieth-century literature and theory, and has produced several studies of postmodernism within the context of Canadian writing.

*Jill LeBihan's* interests are in the field of postcolonial literatures and Canadian writing in particular, on which topics she has given a variety of papers at conferences in Britain and Canada. She is currently teaching at the University of Leeds on completing a doctorate on the representation of nineteenth-century women by contemporary Canadian women writers. She was a Visiting Graduate in the English Department at the University of Alberta from 1989–90.

*Colin Nicholson* is a Senior Lecturer at Edinburgh University where he teaches English, United States and Canadian literature. In 1990 he edited *Margaret Laurence: New Critical Essays* and is now editing a volume on *Margaret Atwood*. At present he is the editor of the *British Journal of Canadian Studies*.

*Rosalie Osmond* has been an Assistant Professor in the English Departments of York University, Toronto, and Mount Allison University. Author of numerous scholarly articles, her book, *Mutual Accusation*, was published by University of Toronto Press in July 1990. She is the current holder of the Charles Douglas-Home Research Award.

*Stephen Regan* is Tutor in Literature at Ruskin College, Oxford. After reading English and American Studies at the University of Hull, he lived in Canada for several years and was a research student at York University and the University of Toronto. He is Associate Editor of *The Year's Work in English Studies* and the author of a book on Philip Larkin.

*David Richards* teaches English and Commonwealth literature at the University of Leeds. He has published a number of articles on post-colonial writing and on anthropology. He is currently writing a book (with Shirley Chew and Lynette Hunter) on new Commonwealth writing and a book entitled *The Masks of Difference* on the relationship of anthropological and literary representations.

*John A. Thieme* is Professor of English at the University of Hull and previously taught at the University of Guyana and the Polytechnic of North London. He is the author of *The Web of Tradition: Uses of Allusion in V. S. Naipaul's Fiction* and has published extensively on Commonwealth writing.

# Acknowledgements

These essays are a collective production of the Literature Group of the British Association for Canadian Studies, and owe much to the constant attention of Peter Easingwood who has chaired the Group in recent years. We would like to thank all those who provided support and ideas for this collection, particularly Michael Hellyer and the Academic Relations Office of the Canadian High Commission and all those institutions which have hosted our meetings and provided academic and administrative help over the last four years.

# Introduction

## Lynette Hunter

The one consistent motif in Canadian studies over the last three decades has been the discussion of the search for 'Canadian identity'. Initially perceived in terms of the need to construct such an identity in the face of an apparently banal culture and apathetic society, recent developments have radically recast the discussion. Contemporary studies view the issue not as the construction of an absent identity, but as the articulation of a distinct identity that has been suppressed by or subject to dominant traditions and conventions from elsewhere, particularly Europe or the United States.

This recasting, along with the emerging relevance of postmodernist strategies – long perceived as typical to Canadian literature – has located in Canadian writings a fruitful setting for the study of literary techniques and devices helpful to the articulation of non-traditional voices outside the mainstream. Unless you can attempt to say who or what you are, you cannot be heard. You have to have both a position to speak from and a voice to speak with.

The essays in this collection are concerned with the parallel strands of colonial and women's writings in Canada over the last two decades. Both strands can be seen as attempts to find a voice amid a set of conventions and traditions which do not necessarily encourage them to speak. The more consciously they foreground the problems of articulation, the more securely these writings situate themselves within postcolonialist and feminist approaches or discourses. While women's search for a different voice has been a consistent strand in Canadian literary history, the postcolonial voice has been a long time surfacing. In some ways the relegation of women to a non-contentious domestic sphere has permitted an exploration of narrative strategies, of varieties of discourse, which would not have been acceptable within the overtly political struggle of colonialism. This is, of course, a matter of perception.

The postcolonial is perceived as more threatening to tradition since it implies a re-examination of structures of power, of the hierarchies of public/personal/ private that in effect puts all people in Canada in a feminist position. In doing so postcolonial writing underlines the compromises and complexities of social organization, not only from the position of those with no voice but also from the position of those who only have a conventional voice. The feminist dilemmas, parallel to but different in emphasis from the postcolonial, are to find a voice without denying it to others. This lies at the heart of feminist politics and at the heart of the compromises feminism makes.

The different stances explored by Canadian writers over the last twenty years have initiated alternative ways of writing. The attempt to find a voice amid sets of conventions and traditions which do not necessarily encourage you to speak raises related issues. To be heard, recognized, permitted to engage actively in the life of a society, you have to speak in the traditional language of that society. Yet this is the very tradition whose conventions and limitations make it difficult for you to speak, and bias what you want to say. The focus of the critical discussions throughout this book is upon the interrelation of realism, modernism and postmodernism as a set of tensions within the literary tradition generated from these social contradictions. The discussions here comment directly upon the current theoretical debate about the need to articulate history within traditional/conventional language and discourse which does not allow for it.

If much of the current debate begins from the position that the premodernist realism of the late-nineteenth or early twentieth century is a stale and overworked convention of representation, then all these essays can be seen as attempts either to reclaim the word 'real' for material history or to reclaim the possibility for historical recounting that lies at the root of a now conventional representative tradition. Modernism can be defined as the articulation of the subject trying to speak of real personal experience. Many developments in modernism do not explicitly address history since they are concerned with the private rather than the public. Furthermore, the tendency of modernism to look inward for self and position can underwrite many of the limiting qualities of fixity, of inviolate essence, that the word 'identity' often calls up. At the same time, on rarer occasions, the modernist look inward, sees nothing. Certainly the most enduring modernist works are at this crossroads of self and nothing. Yet modernism's attempt to lasso the significant moments, those isolated epiphanies of experience where we seem to find ourselves, indicates its residual striving after the unique, the essential.

The development of postmodernism has been double-sided. On the one hand its strategies can be taken as an attempt at a complete severance from history. Such severance is only available to subjects perceiving themselves or being read as within the mainstream literary tradition. Only these subjects can at one and the same time detach themselves from history and still find it possible to speak. It could be said that while they think they are achieving ahistoricity, their medium is inexorably rooted in historical event of which they are consciously or subconsciously choosing to remain unaware. But postmodernism has also claimed the utter necessity of history, the inevitability and significance of social contingency. While both postmodernisms try to fragment the essential identity of modernism, the former instigates a pluralism of games playing which attempts to evade social action. In contrast, the latter attempts to fracture the conventional, expose what is taken for granted, and engage both with the significance of or perceived need for the convention, and with possible different action and articulation appropriate for the present.

The essays here watch the intercommentary between feminist and postcolonial writings as they engage with realism, modernism and postmodernism. In studies of both text and theory they emphasize the strength that each position derives from a historical stance, one that recognizes and stresses the material event.

Emerging into the arguably appropriate generic structures of the short fiction which speaks of isolation or the serial short fiction book with its fractured wholeness, and generic modes of the fictional documentary or autobiography with their precarious identity, the Canadian writings discussed here yield a wide range of narrative strategies for speaking about alterity and difference. Alternative, marginal, writers have consistently turned to fantasy as a stance through which they could speak in opposition to the conventional. In the last two decades women writers in particular have developed a series of generic strands from the fantastic to the utopian/dystopian. It is significant that women in the western world, who have not been denied education or publishing possibilities to the same extent as even more marginalized groups, have turned to a literary form which is deeply rooted in conventional and naturalized communication. Fantasy permits other voices but controls and defines them. It is immensely appropriative, and profoundly supportive of the ideological.

For other alternative voices the attempt is necessarily different, partly because they have learned from the history of fantasy. But further, rather than being controlled or repressed, many of these voices have quite simply been denied. The recent explosion of postcolonial literature into postmodernist techniques of generic disruption, intertextuality and detailed poetic displacements aims, according to the critics in this book, toward the fractured, the nebulous, the delirious. The stances described in these literary forms try to avoid the oppositional, although it is not possible at the moment to assess just how successful the attempt can be, because being in opposition presupposes acceptance of the 'normal' and compromises the writing into the conventional. The postcolonial foregrounds the shortcomings not only of realism but also of fantasy, and the essays on Canadian women's writings that are included, helpfully explore the implications of those shortcomings and assess the developments.

In many ways, the broader significance of Canadian literature from the last two decades for other writing in English may be derived from its problematic engagement with the contradictions between the different strands of post-modernism, its attempt to be apolitical and yet historical at the same time, its insistence on the materiality of personal identity simultaneously with its rejection of the social. The examples of postcolonial and women's writings which are studied here address the contradictions directly. Through them the essayists attempt to retrieve the real, and realism, for historical postmodernism.

*   *   *

The opening contribution to this collection, 'Short fictions and whole books' by Andrew Gurr, discusses the specifically modernist attempt to articulate individual difference or identity through the narrative structure of short fiction, within a world of realism which asks for entrenched convention. Short fiction, with its metaphoric and associative strategies, raises a unique set of problems when a writer chooses to juxtapose a series of such fictions and create a whole book. The wholeness of this set of fictions is difficult to maintain because the formal conventions of the novel can pull it into the linear and the discursive, and can diffuse the intimacy of the individual subjective portrait. Firmly set within a Commonwealth perspective, the essay comments on both the potential and the problems of the whole-book form in Katherine Mansfield's writing, before suggesting that Rudy Wiebe's *Blue Mountains* is one of the few successful attempts. Gurr goes on to study the way that Naipaul, Richler, Laurence and Munro, all moving from the example of Steinbeck's *Cannery Row*, use the 'street' as an informing motif for structuring short fictions into whole books. All of these writers, Laurence in particular, are regional, located in a specific place and history. This historical bias means that they fail to use, or indeed actively reject, the personal alienation, the intensely private epiphanies and the open-endedness of modernist forms. However, while this bias can move the narrative back into the conventions of premodernist realism, the suggestion is made that in shifting the observer's gaze from the inward to the outward, the serial form may prove helpful to the regional voice, may enable the communication of history through strategies of cumulative background. On the one hand those strategies are conventional and obstructive to different identity, while on the other they are a site for the reclamation of different histories.

It is precisely this dilemma faced by the regional writer using strategies of realism that Peter Easingwood addresses in ' Semi-autobiographical fiction and revisionary realism in *A Bird in the House*'. The discussion here opens with the voices of two prairie writers: Margaret Laurence claiming realism as a vital strategy for extending regional identity and Robert Kroetsch arguing that the compulsion to history and regionalism makes necessary a violation of realism. This essay presents Margaret Laurence as looking at the interconnection of literary realism and life through recall and re-telling. The reiteration of event is the process which Laurence calls history. The process is enabled/well served by the serial short fiction structure: the form allows for gaps, discontinuities and breaks not only in the narration of event (the contradictions of memory) but also of narrative perspective (clashes of realism, for example, between the views of child and adult). The resulting genre of the re-told or oft-told tale yields a criticism of the kind of realism that 'takes for granted' an ability transparently to tell the stories of minority peoples, here native people and the Métis. Indeed Easingwood suggests that Laurence's primary concern within her regionalism is with the recognition of people without a voice and the need to help them find one. She simultaneously rejects the commonplace and insists on common experience. In order to articulate common experience, to foreground the need for a realism that actively seeks out a voice for the voiceless, Laurence mingles into it romance, which is interpreted here as the negation of realism in contrast to fantasy which is simply its other face.

The importance of finding a voice, of locating self, place, position, is carried further in 'The tuning of memory: Alistair MacLeod's short fiction' by Colin Nicholson. Here once more it is suggested that what relates life to history is language. In an argument of some elegance, Nicholson brings together a reading of Paul Ricoeur's theory of history and language with a practical reading of Alistair MacLeod's short fictions; this reading anchors and permits discussion of concepts that by definition resist stated explanation. The underlying question concerns the relation between realism and history, which in the post-Renaissance period has come, despite a general recognition of its inadequacy, to connote a referential or essential representative function. History needs language and writing to be recognized as history; it has to be recounted or we cannot communicate it. But the moment you arrest it to tell it, it ceases the movement through time that makes it history. This is parallel to the problem of the recognition of the self as something other than essential identity. Indeed Nicholson claims that the location of self is not possible without a history; but history is not fixed, closed and permanent, rather it is modulated with changing time and circumstance. Therefore the location of self makes necessary the narration of the past in language where memory and recall overlap with linguistic and literary structures.

The study of Macleod's writing leads to the suggestion that the occurrence of historical event need not be referential but intertextual. Intertextuality is the literary device that engages with the overlap and is the primary narrative strategy used by Macleod in his stories. Through it the random contingency of event becomes an iterative structure. Building on this argument the discussion moves on to address the issue of compromise: that we need language to locate history and self, but that the conventions of that language are those constructed by others, for other histories, often histories of oppression and power. Language can be used by others to define us, but may also be used by us to define ourselves. The essay suggests that the particular compromise reached by Macleod's short fictions consists of a process of change and slippage from historical origins, textual certainty and predictable convention. Its intertextuality is a way of writing devoted both to existing within and changing the language. It resists closure, consolation, permanence and seeks to write a continuous present that will articulate self, give voice.

The concern with personal and cultural identity being formed through language becomes in John Thieme's study, 'Historical relations: modes of discourse in Michael Ondaatje's *Running in the Family*', a concern with origins and genealogy, with culture and mythology, and the way in which language connects us to personal history. Ondaatje has long been recognized as a writer who points out the inadequacies of conventional realism with a thoroughgoing post-modernist investigation of language and form. Thieme presents Ondaatje's work not only as a deconstruction of received versions of language and history, but also as a reconstruction into alternative paradigms. Possibly because *Running in the Family* is autobiographical and semi-documentary, the writer is here seen to focus on the problem of arriving at any construction at all. What begins as a personal quest for self becomes, in the shared medium of a text, necessarily familial and public. This quest, this textual journey, becomes a commentary on the fugitive nature of past experience and the impossibility of arriving through discourse at any definitive version of history. Yet the emphasis here is not upon intertextual commentary, but upon generic breakdown at all points of the linguistic and literary medium. The text interpolates snapshots of discourse, minimalist disruptions, essentially unrelated juxtapositions. It combines the oral story-teller with the photographer, the journalist, the poet, and positions the writer, the reader and the text in a kaleidoscope of shifting patterns and interactions. Thieme suggests that on the whole the work seems curiously innocent of politics, that the writing is not really concerned with the brutality of imperialism. However satisfying the narrative may be to those who do not need an alternative history, who appreciate/enjoy the pleasure of the formal post-modernist strategies of the text, there is a sense that here the quest has lost its way, that language has permitted the re-telling but has not connected us to history: a useful reminder that strategies of dislocation do not inevitably tell another history, except perhaps here a history of the inadequacy of traditional structures.

'*Burning down the House*: Neil Bissoondath's fiction', from David Richards, takes on the specific issue of the relation of colonial discourses to post-modernism. The commentary raises profound theoretical questions about the implications of compromise into a system of discourse which at least permits a legitimate voice but provides a circumscribed and misleading political position. It also offers suggestions about the helpfulness of moving out of that compromise and hence also out of an immediately effective political position, while maintaining the possibility for discussion because the voice still speaks.

Taking on early theory from Fanon and recent theory from Homi Bhabha, Richards argues that whereas colonial discourse was originally dialogic, between other voices and the central tradition, it is now a triangulation of different voices that can potentially change the way we read. Working from the suggestion that Canadian literature is based on a recognition that literary conventions from one society are never appropriate to a different place, Bissoondath's work is fundamentally involved in the recognition of art or representation as self-delusion. The novel sets up a traditional narrative of realism and linearity, as well as an evocation of its capacity for misrepresentation and failure. But this is not a banal historical construction of dualism. The tradition and the misrepresentation ironize each other into the terrible comedy of the colonist subject. Bissoondath's postmodernist play, like Ondaatje's, examines the privileges/priorities of myth and narrative which allow the colonial only misrepresentation or negation of self and identity. This dilemma is presented as one not only for the characters but also for the writer: how can narrative escape the bias of convention without fleeing to negation? How can a voice make, but not be in, a narrative? Here the writer develops a detached voice, attempting to give voice to the voiceless in someone else's accents, accents not connected to the historical subject, Bissoondath himself. An array of strategies of omission, disruption and fracture constructs continual ellipses, a 'constellation of delirium' from whose interstices the writer speaks with a voice which has no place in colonialism or realism yet which cannot speak without them.

Extending the problems of colonialism into the multiple marginalities of race, immigrant groups and gender, Shirley Chew's 'One cast of a net: a reading of Daphne Marlatt's *Steveston*', questions how or if one can come to a sense of self/place/voice. Placed alongside Marlatt's poem, *Steveston*, is the documentary form of *Steveston Recollected* in which the writer tries to locate the history of the town in interviews, transcripts, translations, photographs and memory as well as other more conventional devices for narrative description. Yet even the various, multiplicitous form of this document is curiously unsatisfactory. Too much is taken for granted, the voiceless cannot be heard. In contrast, *Steveston* interprets the silences of the documentary, fills the gaps with a voice. To find this voice, Chew follows the poet as she leaps into different discourses in a precarious poetics which overlaps verse and prose, initiates a disruptive play around genre, style and voice, and which dislocates the syntax of language laying open its multiple and conflicting possibilities. This graceful critical activity points first to the negativity of oppositions, to the entrapments and compromises entailed in using and even in ironizing conventional language. Such atrophy is supplanted by a critical poetics that refuses closure, and indicates the spiral movement of *Steveston* toward recognition of self. Certainties are erased, as are oppositions; they are replaced by 'simultitude'. Particularly rewarding, the poetics of both the critic and the poet are firmly positioned on a historical basis. Chew's presentation of *Steveston* foregrounds the oppositional qualities of the first and second generation Japanese–Canadians, who are tied to traditional accounts of history. Against the vision of the *issei* and *nisei*, are set present-day Japanese–Canadians, who look to the terrain and its material contingency. Marlatt is like these *sansei*, a voice that finds self in articulating the real, the simultitude of place, of the immediacy of our social history.

Far more uneasy with the potential in language and profoundly distrustful of genre is Coral Ann Howells' reading of Marian Engel: 'On gender and writing: Marian Engel's *Bear* and *The Tattooed Woman*'. Engel is shown to move between the conventional presentations of woman's life in realism and the promise of realized personal desire in fantasy, as a way of articulating female experience. *Bear* moves between the two, mixing the genres, disrupting their pattern to indicate that both are seductions into the ideological and usual. It is only in the brief moment between the two, when realism is supplanted by the irrational, the magical, the mystical, that we can peer through to the other side. Whereas *Bear* moves to a recognizably too easy mystic communion, the narratives of *The Tattooed Woman* leave one with an uneasy oddness. These short fictions write about the need to use all available conventions, to find the discontinuities between the real and the writing available to expressing that reality: not only the literary but the daily, the mundane ephemera of lives, even the physical body if that is the only medium left to a woman to try to speak about herself. As the narrators in these stories move from one convention to another, it is the movement itself which seems to enable the articulation of fundamentally strange and different obsessions, fears, rages and passions. There is a sense that the group of short stories generates a mosaic of genres and of social pattern, where the pieces only roughly fit together, and where actual experience – the voice of Engel's women – may come only from the irregular joins or spaces that lie along the edges of the pieces.

The need to move beyond the immediate oppositions of realism and fantasy is paralleled in the 'Arrangements, "Disarrangements", and "Earnest Deceptions" ' of Rosalie Osmond's title. This contribution studies a development in Alice Munro's short fiction style from the patterns and arrangements that provide her characters with their sense of self to the disarrangements of *Who Do You Think You Are?* and *The Moons of Jupiter*. Osmond argues that Munro increasingly finds life and reality random. Its disarrangements function as epiphanies that disturb what is taken for granted and call individuals to find their own patterns and rearrangements. Yet this tension between order and disorder, between rejection of and desire for romance begins to suggest the possibility that just as with reality and fantasy, both arrangements and rearrangements are earnest deceptions. Munro's later work, including the title story of *The Progress of Love*, shows a shift in emphasis away from personal rearrangements, to a living with different versions of the real that is artful but does not look to satisfy a desire for pattern and significance. The critic here indicates that the modernist epiphany can be a problem for a marginal writer, a writer from a minority position, because it posits a possible solution to or revelation of identity and even if it is transcendent, such action suggests compromise, points to an earnest deception.

The commentaries by Howells and Osmond also hint at why the fragmentation of postmodernism is so attractive or helpful to writers outside mainstream traditions, here women, because other modes can more easily be reconstructed as compromise. Postmodernism can emphasize the fracture, not just foreground the difference which indicates as significant something that others may have thought of as banal, but difference which indicates the rifts in ideology, the places where there is no voice yet there is a person. This strategy describes not liberal plurality which uses the deconstructive techniques of post-structuralism and postmodernism to allow for a number of voices somehow all existing side by side, but instead a position that recognizes that any ideology will disadvantage someone – there is always a marginalized someone deprived of adequate voice. In these essays postmodernist strategies become a political tool both to indicate the disadvantaged and to give it voice or space.

The different strands in postmodernism are outlined in Jill LeBihan's study of Margaret Atwood's recent novels, 'Feminist? Futures?'. Here the differences are cast in terms of the prefix 'post': first as signifying a response to something that has passed into the past, then as an indication of contemporaneity and plurality of voice, and lastly as the edge feature, the delimiting conditions of which we become aware as we shuttle between past and present, and which attains its positivity through attention to history. The argument put forward is that to read *The Handmaid's Tale* or *Cat's Eye* as oppositions of realism and fantasy, of feminism and postfeminism, is to cast them into either/or positions which do not encourage the articulation of anything outside the already-defined or accepted. Furthermore LeBihan suggests that both novels insist on a conscious awareness of historical event which jogs personal memory into recognizing the inadequacy of such either/or positions. History is far more complicated that this and always indicates the positions which are defined or encompassed by neither but which emerge along their limits as edge features. *The Handmaid's Tale* plays with the generic oppositions of social utopia and private fantasy, and stretches them with the disrupting features of memory, autobiography, confession. Within the strongly defined ideological voice from which she is specifically excluded, the narrator attempts to locate a self through illicit acts of memory which construct alternative histories. But what is significant about those histories is not that they are true but that they show up the edge features that elude both official and individual definitions. The more subtle oppositions of conventional and personal realisms in *Cat's Eye* find edge features in the constructions of the dimension of time, as the past infuses the present.

Atwood's emphatic message is that we can arrange and can be arranged, but we can also helpfully indicate edge features as long as we remain aware of history. Her writing focuses on the differences for the marginalized not only as subjects but also as objects. The compromises of language are not only personal but also public. Nothing happens if you do not attempt to speak, and you have a responsibility to do so. There is a further responsibility not to include the marginalized as such in the compromise of speech and writing, but to indicate it only in the edge features. Atwood's feminism is here presented as to do with indicating or drawing the edge features of womens' position. As such it eludes definition of fixed identity; it functions as a location through which, not from or at which, we may act politically on behalf of a particular marginality.

The final essay in the collection is ' "The presence of the past": modernism and postmodernism in Canadian short fiction' contributed by Stephen Regan. Gathering up several strands from the discussions both of colonialism and feminism, the essay claims that historical and political postmodernism is a defining literary response from Canadian writers to their historical circumstances. As David Richards' contribution also notes, Canadian writing may be presented as continually self-conscious about reference and representation, this self-consciousness immediately problematizes the status of history and fiction, as well as the manner in which identity is represented. Regan depicts several short fiction writers, focusing on Laurence, Gallant and Munro, as worried about the ideological underpinning of realism, the way it takes too much for granted and appears to obstruct the personal and public questioning of self and action. Yet each also avoids the autonomous ground, the isolation of modernism. The short fiction form provides a narrative strategy for a subtle play of the relationship between traditional history and private memory. Gallant's shifts in memory perspective probe possibilities for political action in their sceptical exposure of social and historical determinants. Laurence uses lies, secrets and deceptions to emphasize the discrepancy between public and personal memory; her realism repeatedly fractures, destabilizes and disorders the conventional. Munro's intensely self-reflexive questionings of historicity seek not truth but the delicate adjustments of significance and in doing so invite the reader into the process. Regan ends with a brief look at developments into postmodernist fabulation and historiographic metafiction in writings by Audrey Thomas and Rudy Wiebe. Canadian writers emerge as defined by their response to the distortions of conventional historiography, their writing finding identity in their rewriting of history from the point of view of the dispossessed.

Each of these essays studies the particular problem of self-definition for people who live outside mainstream culture and identity and the need to locate and articulate self, place and position in order to be seen and to be heard. They respond to the contemporary debate about an a/historical postmodernism by reclaiming the techniques for historical narrative from realism and challenging its conventional stance. These critics portray recent Canadian writing as sabotaging traditional identities, as writing which overtly presents the over-written world of private memory, collective region, and personal history. Through strategies which gain particular strength from the extended juxtapositions of parallel texts, intertextuality, serial fiction, generic mixing and disruption, all deny an easy coherence at the same time as they claim a narrative. The critics here look for and sometimes find the location for a repressed or denied voice in the interstices of mosaic, fracture, rift, simultaneity, edge feature, ellipsis. The techniques of the postmodern are subjected to scrutiny as these writers discard its plurality and insist on history.

# 1

# Short Fictions and Whole-Books

## Andrew Gurr

My tour is from Katherine Mansfield's Burnell or 'Karori' stories, through Naipaul's *Miguel Street* via Mordecai Richler's *The Street*, with a detour into Rudy Wiebe's *Blue Mountains*, and a peep at *The Bird in the House*, to end up at Alice Munro's *Lives of Girls and Women* and *The Beggar Maid*: a conducted tour of a far from orchestrated chorus of writers of short fiction. The conductor of such a tour has to take account of the peculiar problems of form that all these books offer. The problems are not just the basic one which faces any collection of short stories, which William Sansom compared to the incompatibility of paintings seen side by side in an art gallery. 'Short stories in book form', he wrote, 'like pictures in galleries, create bad habits: read or seen one after the other they cancel themselves out.'[1] The collections of short stories I have listed here on the whole do the opposite. By their juxtapositioning, and by the fact that they use the same raw materials in each story – a family, a street, a community or a small town – the stories augment one another and actively inhibit the process of selecting and isolating each artefact, each story, as Sansom feels the form requires. Their problem is that they lose their separate identity as short stories through that juxtaposition, and therefore become something else, more like a discontinuous set of chapters from a novel, and yet not a novel. They are a distinct, and I would go so far as to say distinctly peculiar, genre of their own. They meet the aesthetic requirements neither of short fiction nor of the novel.

This is a problem largely because the modernist short story has its own distinctive aesthetic, incompatible with that of the novel. These unified collections have the classic problem, or possibly we should think of it as the domestic problem, of falling between two stools. A subtitle for this chapter might be 'the problematic aesthetics of the whole-book'. That name I take from Ken Thompson's definition as he composed it for *A Bird in the House*: 'Whole-book: a book which is more than a collection of short stories and yet, although like a novel in some ways, not a novel'.[2] If it is more than a collection of short stories and yet not a novel, it must have an aesthetic and formal character of its own. My object here is to look at the nature of that distinctive aesthetic character, and to wonder out loud whether it is not a hybrid, a mule. We all know what the fertility rate of mules is.

The honour, if that is what it is, of originating the 'whole-book' concept lies with Katherine Mansfield, that unacknowledged legislator of modernist short fiction. 'Prelude' and 'At the Bay' were conceived more or less together, deal with the same family of characters and use the identical twelve-cell symbolist structure to present a kind of before and after link – Linda Burnell, afraid of both pregnancy and the flowering of the self in 'Prelude', and her astonishing reconciliation with the baby which has arrived in the meantime, in 'At the Bay'. For all that cohesion the two stories were actually written more than five years apart, and each of them became the first story in separate collections which highlight different stories in their titles-: 'Prelude' opens *Bliss and other Stories*, and 'At the Bay' opens *The Garden Party*. Mansfield had, when she died, written a third story about the Burnells, 'The Doll's House', planned like the others as the first story in her next collection, *The Dove's Nest*; but this one appeared post-humously. She wrote no other stories about the Burnells, and it is a teasing question whether death or some more aesthetic impediment got in the way of this whole-book or novel or set of discontinuous episodes which for years she planned and wanted to publish as an ostensible novel called *Karori*.

'The Doll's House' does, I think, indicate some of the possible impediments which got in the way of the *Karori* collection. 'Prelude' is centred, as in their different ways all these whole-books are, on childish discovery, the early learn-ing process. It has as an off-centre focal figure Kezia, the child who undergoes the transformation into the new house in the Wellington suburb of Karori and who explores its garden and its aloe in the story. She is aged perhaps four. The second story, a year later, would put her at five. 'The Doll's House', the last of the three, has her as a small child at school, probably six or seven. At what point, Mansfield must have wondered, should this process of innocent learning and discovery stop? She had already written a group of stories about adolescent discovery, focused on Laura Sheridan in 'The Garden Party', and was distinctly aware of the differences between the kinds of story appropriate for early child-hood and those for adolescence. The latter kind she found 'too easy', fit for the common market she supplied in *The Sphere* but not for the real development of her art, which she applied above all in the Karori stories. The adolescent stories have a linear structure, are more orthodox in their discursive function as narra-tive than the twelve cells of the major symbolist fictions, 'Prelude', 'At the Bay' and 'The Daughters of the Late Colonel'. 'The Doll's House' also has a linear narrative and, superb story though it is, I think that it must have warned Mansfield that she was stretching her whole-book concept of discrete, discontinuous cells of narrative and their associative symbolism too far. She remained dissatisfied with the ending of the linear 'Garden Party', partly, I think, because she was too caught up in the modernist prose fiction mode of plotless stories which have, and should have, no ending.

The associative technique that goes with the twelve-cell structure runs all too quickly into problems of scale. The words most used in this century for modernist short fiction – fragmentation, snapshot photography, the cameo – with its uniqueness and fleetingness, and the 'high excitement' which Poe said was the necessarily transient accompaniment of the short story or poem (long before Ezra Pound he said a long poem was a paradox): all these indicate the brevity essential to the form. The parallels and contrasts of associationism, brilliantly exploited in the twelve sections of 'Prelude' and 'At the Bay', cannot survive much elongation. To lengthen the form required a different kind of narrative, more linear, as in 'The Doll's House' and 'The Garden Party'. *Karori* as a finished whole-book could never, I think, have satisfied Mansfield's demanding aesthetic criteria. It would have demanded in the end too much of the linear structuring which 'The Doll's House' imposed on her.

That is a contentious assertion which I cannot develop substantially here, where the main subject is Canadian writing. I can instead point, with a discreet piece of self-advertisement, to a different but equivalent version of the same problem posed by Rudy Wiebe's *The Blue Mountains of China*. Wiebe's book began, rather like *Karori*, as a collection of quite separate stories about the Mennonite brethren among whom Wiebe was born and raised. In his own account of the book's inception he said:

> I simply got ideas for stories which, at the time, I had no sense were going to be of any particular pattern put together. I thought of a cycle, maybe a series, of stories about the Mennonites wherever they might be.[3]

In its final form, however, the book is usually read as a novel, and the full structure, a gradual convergence on the culminating Chapter 13, is vastly more coherent than any assembly or collection of separate stories. I have written before about the technical complexities of this (hence my use of Wiebe as evidence for the whole-book problem, and the self-advertisement). What I shall do here is briefly summarize the main point and then go on to apply it to all the other whole-books I mentioned at the beginning.

The essential problem is one of formal structure. In the more linear mode of narrative, as in a novel or a traditional tale, or an anecdotal short story, the form is metonymic, discursive, making all the necessary connections explicit. In the symbolist mode of what has been called 'short fiction' as distinct from the 'short story' of the other mode, the characteristic form is metaphoric, associative, non-linear, leaving all the connections inexplicit or at most implicit. It is the mode of poetry rather than the novel. It was Katherine Mansfield's fictional mode and led her to call 'Prufrock' 'after all, a short story' and led Eliot to heap praise on the symbolist elegances of 'Bliss'. The most obvious quick way of differentiating the two modes as short story or short fiction is by looking at their endings. Short stories end with the punch-line of a joke or the point that you expect from an anecdote. Short fictions have no endings. 'Prelude' just stops. 'At the Bay''s twelfth cell reaches the end of the day which dawned in the first cell, and stops.

The difficulty of combining these two modes is exemplified in *The Blue Mountains of China*. Each chapter, each story – or short fiction – ends indeterminately, with no evident or obvious point. Only as the stories accumulate, and cross-linkages of people and place can be made, does a linear structure begin to emerge. By the thirteenth chapter, or story, the whole-book structure has made it impossible to read it in isolation as another independent if associated short fiction. The different tracks taken by the different Mennonite groups and individuals finally merge, by an obviously fortuitous accident, on a roadside in middle Canada in the bicentenary year 1976. Points are asking to be made. This no longer short fiction has to have an ending. So it must follow, as the night the day – darkness after light – that the symbolist, associative mode of the separate stories is drawn up, or out, or down, into the metonymy of the novel. I have argued in an article called '*Blue Mountains* and Strange Forms'[4] that Wiebe creates a strange merger of the two modes in his final chapter and I will not go back into that now. What I should like to do instead is look at some of the other collections which fall into this hybrid, possibly mulish form, and consider what kind of fertility the merger offers the writers who use it.

If there is a classic in this mode it must be Steinbeck's *Cannery Row*. Steinbeck used the setting of the Monterey fishwharves as the base for a series of single stories about single characters. Each one was a discontinuous, discrete unit. The cohesion is one of accumulation rather than augmentation. The characters in each story are seen from outside, the repeated use of the same setting allowing some economies in the description of the setting and occasionally a lead into the next story in the sequence. It is not really a sequence or a whole-book; though it does cohere. I think it evades rather adroitly the problem William Sansom identified, of the stories cancelling each other out. But it does have something of the *Spoon River Anthology*'s air about it, of an anthropologist's study of a set of gravestones.

A little closer to home, if that is what Canada is, lies Naipaul's *Miguel Street*. Inspired by *Cannery Row*, it has the same economy of setting, though it deals far more intensively with its characters and makes a much more cohesive point about them. It is without doubt a whole-book, and a brilliantly constructed one. The narrator is an eye, and an 'I', and the sequence of stories follows the young narrator's discovery process in a beautifully elegant, diffuse but tightly controlled way. Each story about each character, as in Steinbeck, is wholly self-sufficient. What grows on the reader, as it grows in the narrator, is cumulative, a series of cases. They all, in oblique ways (gradually, like Wiebe's whole-book, draw a set of perspective lines to the conjoint themes of escape and fantasy) escape into fantasy, the delusion of escape through scholarship or through fantasy itself. Some of the stories, like 'B. Wordsworth', direct our attention to the more serious form of fantasy called creativity; but the narrator who is the author never makes a point of this portrait being of the artist as a young man. Not until the final chapter does the narrator serve as more than an observer. Rather it is the demolition of fantasies, including in the end that of the father figure for the boys of the street, and the final convergence of exploitative fantasy into Ganesh with the reality of escape on a scholarship. The same themes run through all the stories, but only by association can we identify them and only by the cumulative process of the boy growing and discovering can the stories arrive at a conclusion which gives shape and identity to the ostensibly random, anecdotal tales which have gone before. Technically the achievement, the merger of epiphanic or symbolist short fiction with the larger linear structure of the novel, is very close to Wiebe's, though in Naipaul it is much less obviously a single structure. Wiebe's lines converge on the final chapter. Naipaul's tales, or chapters, progress in a simpler linear fashion, without the architecture or the artifice or the demand for sheer hard work in identifying the linkages which Wiebe lays on his reader.

In these three examples, in Mansfield, Wiebe and Naipaul, I think we have demonstrations both of the problem inherent in the form of the whole-book and two relatively successful attempts to cope with it and exploit the strengths of (to revert to an earlier metaphor) sitting on either stool. The three other Canadian writers I listed at the beginning all, it seems to me, make less use of the opportunities, and produce lesser works in their 'whole-books' as a consequence.[5]

Mordecai Richler's *The Street* need not hold us – I would say could not as well as should not – for long. The stories are a random gathering, unified by the St Urbain Street which gave birth to Duddy Kravitz; they have none of the cohesion, even growth in the narrator, that strengthen the other whole-books. *Cannery Row* again inspires the idea, modified by the addition of a child narrator who participates in the tales of youth and age. Youth and age in different ways are its two strengths. Age, as in Steinbeck, implies people of fixed personality and habits, who can be captured forever in a single snapshot or pseudo-epiphany. Youth implies discovery, the instant of growth which also depends, like the snapshots of age, on a pseudo-epiphany, a revelatory moment when a new truth dawns and life is made different ever after. In both kinds of story the ostensible epiphany, characteristic of symbolist, associative, modernist short fiction, is really anecdotal narrative, metonymy standing in for metaphor and limited in its possibilities by the distortion it imposes on its narrative form. The stories in *The Street* all have semi-endings, like all good anecdotal New Yorker fiction; but the book as a whole has no end. This, I would claim, is the reverse of what either of the original forms requires.

Now we move to *A Bird in the House*, the collection for which the term whole-book was coined, and which it seems to me is rather less than the sum of its parts. It is, as Peter Easingwood has noted, about discovery, like Mansfield's *Karori* stories, *Miguel Street* and even Richler's *The Street*, a subject well suited to modernist techniques of presentation. But Laurence's book is distinctly pre-modernist. To start with, it is narrated in the first person and the first person, Vanessa, is squarely in the centre of the book. This has a number of conse-quences. First, the extended stretches of narrative description place Vanessa as the first observer of what she describes, well clear of her ostensible subject. She is relating a memoir from twenty years ago, with all the detachment and intensity of distanced scrutiny which that entails. Much more to the point, this detachment removes any possibility of the portrait of the author as a young discoverer which is central in both Mansfield and Naipaul. What this loses Laurence is, of course, the whole apparatus of reflexivity, and the explicit subjectivity which is the chief prerequisite of modernism. The main conse-quence of this modest traditionalism is that the focus shifts from Vanessa to Grandfather Connor and the setting of Manawaka. This in turn makes Laurence emphatically a regional, almost historical, novelist. The discovery process, the growth of the young consciousness, is that of a historian, not a creative artist. The narrative becomes, with Vanessa as the central consciousness, a historian's gradual discovery of the deeper realities beneath the surface. Grandfather Connor's tyranny becomes a consequence (and a cause) of his pioneering origins, Vanessa's difficulties become adjustments to social determinism, the discovery of self as an integral part of the social origins. There is much more objective historical narrative in *A Bird in the House* than there is awakening authorial consciousness. The typology is not modernist.

Alice Munro is far less of a historian than Margaret Laurence. Her two books with one central adolescent figure in all the stories are intriguingly different from each other as well as from *A Bird in the House*. *Lives of Girls and Women*'s first-person narrator, Del Jordan, has a childhood which follows a similar discovery process to Vanessa's, while *The Beggar Maid*'s third-person Rose travels much further and makes a whole person, if not a whole-book. *Lives of Girls and Women*, however, has none of the sequential learning episodes which mark Vanessa's progress through *A Bird in the House*. Its progress is by accu-mulation rather than sequential learning, cumulative experiences, people, episodes, far less tightly bound to the house and its bird than Laurence's book. None the less I would claim Munro as a historian, too, and for reasons which bring me to the point I have to make if this essay is to be a short story and not a short and open-ended fiction.

In an interview with Graeme Gibson in 1973 Munro spoke of growing up alienated from her community of prairie farmers:

> Perhaps it helps to grow up feeling very alienated from the environment you happen to live in . . . I grew up in a rural community, a very tradi-tional community. I almost always felt it. I find it still when I go back. The

concern of everyone else I knew was dealing with life on a very practical level, and this is very understandable, because my family are farmers, and they are two or three generations away from being pioneers ... but I always realised that I had a different view of the world, and one that would bring me into great trouble and ridicule if it were exposed.[6]

Del Jordan feels this much more strongly than Vanessa, though still with nowhere near the subjective intensity of Kezia in 'The Doll's House'. That kind of intensity is one of the losses sustained by the extension into a whole-book structure.

I would put together Munro's point about feeling alien in home territory and Laurence's historian observer role to emphasize the extent to which all these fictions, all the longer ones – I include Wiebe but exclude Mansfield – share a consciousness of regional identity which makes it impossible for them to take on with any real intimacy the subjective portrait of the author-as-young-discoverer role for which Joyce invented and Mansfield developed plotless short fiction, the epiphany and the open ending. Instead the regional short story becomes, when collected into books in the way Naipaul, Wiebe, Laurence, Richler and Munro have done, a kind of anthropological exercise. The young observer is looking outwards, not inwards. We need not be surprised that this characteristic of regionalism should spread to even the larger metropolitan societies, where poverty generates a sense of region. Pat Barker's *Union Street*, published in 1982 about a region not a vast distance from the back parts of Coronation Street, has exactly the same whole-book format, too.

I am not saying that the historical or anthropological mode is inferior to modernist short fiction. I am saying that it is essentially different, different in its metonymic mode, its outsider audience, its inherently novelistic impulses. Those differences in part explain why it has grown up as a hybrid, starting from the self-discovery of the epiphany and the plotless story and turning almost involuntarily into a narrative; descriptive, sometimes sequential and linear, sometimes more randomly cumulative. I maintain that *Blue Mountains* is the only masterpiece in this hybrid mode and I would argue that few subjects could fit into the kind of structure which Wiebe contrived for that whole-book. By implication and comparison other attempts at whole-books, in so far as they do attempt the massive coherence of a novel, are lesser creations. Perhaps we should be more willing to value short fictions and short stories for what they can do on their own. And so with novels, experimental or traditional. The true strength of these whole-books, Laurence's and Munro's, is not that they are whole-books, a distinctive hybrid with a genetic strength of its own, but rather that they are novels with a built-in fragmentation which lends them the illusion of modernism, though without the real strengths of the modernist, plotless form.

I might go further and argue, too tendentiously perhaps, that the plotless story, the form of modernist short fiction, is hostile to truly regional writing. If you are a regional writer – as for all their disavowals of Canadianness these Manitobans and Ontarians certainly are – you are impelled to provide a quantum of description, of explanation, however tacit, to intensify the observer status which younger writers commonly adopt; and the whole-book mode is characteristic of earlier writing in all these cases apart from Wiebe. It is a rare young and regional writer who can manage without the sense of a separate region and a separate identity, with its consequent descriptions for the implied reader-outsider. Mansfield did it, after ten years soaked in post-impressionist metropolitan thinking. More curiously I think other writers creating inside their regions sometimes do it (Keri Hulme is perhaps one). But they usually do so in poetry. I think Wiebe, as a Mennonite in an alien Canadian region, does it. But I do not think the Manitobans and Ontarians are able to stand outside their sense of a regional identity in that way.

On the other hand you might argue that regionalism intensifies the observer status which goes with short fiction, the 'point of illumination', as Katherine Govier has called it. You might also argue that the collection of street (or in Govier's case, avenue) stories provides information in the cumulative back-ground of the juxtaposed stories. There are potential strengths in every form.

## Notes

1  William Sansom, *The London Magazine*, September 1966, p. 10.
2  Kent Thompson, review of *A Bird in the House*, *The Fiddlehead*, 84, 1970, pp. 108–11.
3  Rudy Wiebe, interview with Robert Kroetsch and Shirley Neuman *A Voice in the Land*, ed. W.J. Keith, NeWest Press, Edmonton, 1980, p. 228.
4  *Journal of Commonwealth Literature*, 17, 1982, pp. 153–60.
5  The prevalence of the whole-book as a form in Canada may owe something to Malcolm Lowry's example. He certainly believed in its possibilities. In a letter to James Stern written in Vancouver, he claimed 'It is possible to compose a satisfactory work of art by the simple process of writing a series of good short stories, complete in themselves, good if held up to the light, water-tight if held upside down but full of effects and dissonances that are impossible in a short story, never the less having its purity of form, a purity that can be achieved only by the born short story writer . . .' (*Selected Letters*, ed. Harvey Breit and Margerie Lowry, Philadelphia, Lippincott Press, p. 28).
6  Alice Munro, interview with Graeme Gibson, *Eleven Canadian Novelists*, Toronto, Anansi, 1973, p. 246.

# 2

# Semi-autobiographical Fiction and Revisionary Realism in *A Bird in the House*[1]

**Peter Easingwood**

Realistic fiction, David Lodge has argued, 'works by concealing the art by which it is produced and invites discussion in terms of ethics and thematics rather than poetics and aesthetics.'[2] Margaret Laurence's attitude towards her own writing tends to confirm this view. Her work leaves the critic uneasy over the problem which Lodge's statement implies: that such a mode of vision appears to grant a higher priority to the content of a novel than to its form. Laurence has characteristically asserted that 'theorizing, by itself, is meaningless in connection with fiction.'[3] But she has been ready to comment in detail on the ethical and thematic interest of her novels. Above all, her comments convey a deep respect for realism, for the novel as a medium which continues to represent the ordinary experiences of daily life. Perhaps her strongest conviction and most emphatic claim is represented by the simple statement that 'There is a lot of history in my fiction.'[4] The distrust of 'theorizing' and the assimilation of fiction to history indicate an uncompromising commitment to a realistic procedure. This commitment, which deserves closer analysis, is most evident in the collection of stories *A Bird in the House*, described by the author as 'the only semi-autobiographical fiction I have ever written.'[5]

Laurence's whole approach to narrative fiction may appear the inevitable extension of her strong sense of regional identity. In conversation with fellow Western Canadian writer Robert Kroetsch, she chose to speak of a 'compulsion to set down our background'.[6] Yet for Kroetsch himself, speaking as a novelist and critic, a similar commitment to regional definition absolutely requires the *violation* of 'certain traditional kinds of realism'. From this point of view the realistic novel is certainly no longer writable and is hardly even readable. The idea that fiction can conceal the art by which it is produced must now be rejected as an outrageous imposition on the reader. When Laurence continues to emphasize realism as a criterion for fiction, she apparently betrays an out-dated and naive conception of her business as a novelist. She ends her dialogue with Kroetsch by remarking that: 'Fiction relates to life in a very real way'; as though that effectively closed the discussion.[7]

Nevertheless the interview between Laurence and Kroetsch confirmed their agreement that, as Western Canadian writers, they were 'involved in making a new literature out of a new experience'. The insistence on a new approach appears especially in emphasis throughout their fiction on the 'rediscovery' or 'retelling' of kinds of story which have already become traditional to prairie life. This kind of development is more easy to identify in Kroetsch's writing than in Laurence's. Yet if his determinedly anti-realistic, parodic style of fiction repre-sents one pole of the new writing, then her renewed commitment to realism represents the other. The compulsion to find a new standpoint from which to present Western experience informs her realism, even when its limits seem most sharply restrictive, as in the special case of *A Bird in the House*.

The story of a child growing up on the prairies during the Depression has been retold so often that it has become part of an assumed tradition of Western writing. A paperback blurb quotes the *Vancouver Sun*'s recommendation: 'When Mrs Laurence approaches this oft-told tale she breathes fresh life into it.' But the cliché of resuscitating a dying tradition conveys a misleading and dis-couraging idea of the book. The stories as Laurence actually tells them propose anything but a resigned acceptance of regional myth. On the contrary, the narrative as a whole demonstrates an icy comprehension of the types of story people often like to tell themselves or others: stories of an assumed popular interest which have to do with pioneering; Scots or Irish ancestry; the outdoor life; Indians; the Depression; and the two World Wars. This material is pre-dictably part of the narrative, but the medium through which these aspects of regional history are presented is not one of an easily assumed, transparent realism. Very much part of the experience that the stories convey is the sense of the deliberate effort of reconstruction, by the narrator, which goes into the telling. Predictable features of prairie life are given only grudging recogni-tion. Laurence's style of narrative shows itself constantly hostile to the oft-told tale.

The stories carefully avoid any attempt at a large narrative sweep. Instead they persistently foreground gaps in knowledge, inconsistent reports and breaks in narrative continuity. The following passage on the Depression, though very differently from Kroetsch's humorous and satirical treatment of prairie folklore in *The Words of My Roaring*, works in its own way to illustrate the limitations of local awareness (p. 136):

The Depression did not get better, as everybody had been saying it would. It got worse, and so did the drought. That part of the prairies where we lived was never dustbowl country. The farms around Manawaka never had a total crop failure, and afterwards, when the drought was over, people used to remark on this fact proudly, as though it had been due to some virtue or special status, like the children of Israel being afflicted by Jehovah but never in any real danger of annihilation. But although Manawaka never knew the worst, what it knew was bad enough. Or so I learned later. At the time I saw none of it. For me, the Depression and drought were external and abstract, malevolent gods whose names I secretly learned although they were concealed from me, and whose evil I sensed only superstitiously, knowing they threatened us but not how or why. What I really saw was only what went on in our family.

The child Vanessa is a sensitive observer of the individual lives and relationships around her: the range and power of the stories is enhanced by the fact that her field of vision is shaken by disturbances she could not have explained at the time. Even so, scenes included in 'The Loons', 'The Half-Husky' and the title story show that what is referred to here simply as personal or family experience is strongly marked by the general crisis of the times. The narrative point of view incorporates a strong sense of historical irony arising from the gradual realization of what differences the Depression had made to people's lives.

The text plainly deals with an environment and form of received wisdom already familiar in prairie literature: a Scots–Irish Protestant morality with its classic opposition between duty and love, work and sexuality, the 'upright' good and the 'downright' bad. Laurence's attitude towards this frame of mind is suggested in one of the stories by the ironic application of the title, 'To Set Our House in Order'. Vanessa's narrative questions this conception of order and the sources of authority which dictate it. From the opening description of Grandfather Connor's Brick House onwards, as the Manawaka scene is set, the images of that order are nakedly exposed. The concluding story, 'Jericho's Brick Battlements', connotes by its title the end of an era. The effect of Laurence's writing is not to perpetuate a traditional view of prairie life but to show where the sequence of experience put together in the course of Vanessa's recollections comes into conflict with what used to pass as received opinion. Jarring particulars are remembered as well as the kind of general statements which reflect traditional or anonymous sources of authority. The older Vanessa, herself now a mother, catches herself out using the proverbial sayings or 'clichés of affection' (p. 207) which her own mother had used to her. The effects most strongly foregrounded in the language of the stories suggest the brash, colloquial realism of a child's point of view. Sometimes metaphor is used to dramatize this point of view, as when Vanessa reports: 'I felt, as so often in the Brick House, that my lungs were in danger of exploding, that the pressure of silence would become too great to be borne.' (p. 66) In the final story, the same metaphoric pressure arises in the incident of the furnace fire which, to the perception of everyone but Grandfather Connor, threatens the house itself. The style is consistently deflationary and yet capable at the same time of generating strong tension.

*A Bird in the House* shows strong novelistic potential but the volume actually achieves a form which comes somewhere between the compact dramatic expression of a series of short stories and the more extended narrative interest of a novel. The stories were conceived from the beginning as a series, Laurence has told us. On the other hand, each story is self-contained: 'definitely a short story and not a chapter from a novel.' Yet the total effect becomes 'not unlike a novel'.[8] The ambiguity of this conception accords with the tentative and exploratory nature of the work. Nevertheless the selection of thematic material included in *A Bird in the House*, though centred on domestic scenes and developed on the basis of the oft-told tale, anticipates the wider social and historical scope of *The Diviners*, the novel which follows next in order of composition and which is Laurence's most ambitious work. The narrative voice of Vanessa MacLeod, like that of Morag Gunn in *The Diviners*, recalls and revises the history of her own experience, looking back over a period of twenty years' absence from Manawaka. In the stories, the significance of events is essentially realized at a subliminal level in the consciousness of the narrator as the child she then was, while a more critical adult perspective is implied rather than stated. Vanessa's attitude to her own early experience is no less strongly revisionary than Morag's, though her presence as a character is reserved until the point where she directly intervenes at the end.

The peculiarly introverted but powerfully dramatic development of *A Bird in the House* is illustrated by its approach to a subject which was to become of increasing concern to Laurence: the history of the Métis and the memory of their cultural dispossession in favour of a new generation of English-speaking settlers of Protestant background. The album of Métis songs collected at the end of *The Diviners* testifies to the sincerity of the tribute which the author pays to a people whose way of life once represented a radically different form of society from the one which the eventual settlement of the prairies had created. However *A Bird in the House* deals most directly with the experience of those belonging to the social order which has conspicuously triumphed. Vanessa MacLeod, the narrator and subject of these stories, is seen as the restless child of a family in which standards are still set by the founders of Manawaka itself, the grandparents' generation. When reminded that her Grandfather Connor was a pioneer, Vanessa at once abandons her juvenile attempt at writing a romance of pioneer life: the prospect of romance is spoiled by this confrontation with the known reality. Vanessa's subsequent contact with the Métis girl Piquette Tonnerre then further undermines her confidence in her own background and outlook without providing the new friendship for which she naively hoped: the difference between them is such that Piquette cannot begin to respond to the advances of a middle class child like Vanessa. In a review of George Woodcock's biography of the Métis hero Gabriel Dumont, Laurence herself acknowledges the barrier of prejudice which had still to be overcome in the attitude of her contemporaries:

'There are many ways in which those of us who are not Indian or Métis have not yet earned the right to call Gabriel Dumont ancestor. But I do so, all the same. His life, his legend, and his times are a part of our past which we desperately need to understand and pay heed to.'[9]

In the story, this enlargement of experience occurs only in the narrator's retrospective view of her relationship with the unlucky Métis girl. But this suggestion of desperate need provides a key to the romance which underlies the realism of these stories. The Métis connection in this particular story brings into focus a pattern of romance of which variations occur throughout the volume and which illustrates a psychological compulsion.

In 'The Loons', Piquette is described as a 'half-breed'. The narrative introduces the Tonnerre family as a familiar part of the local scene, though they are treated as outcasts by the rest of the community (p. 115):

They were, as my grandfather MacLeod would have put it, neither flesh, fowl nor good salt herring . . . Sometimes old Jules, or his son Lazarus, would get mixed up in a Saturday night brawl, and would hit out at whoever was nearest, or howl drunkenly among the offended shoppers on Main Street, and the Mountie would put them for the night in the barred cell underneath the Court House, and the next morning they would be quiet again.

The narrative code which introduces the Métis always soon relapses into silence. The proposal that Vanessa's doctor–father makes to take Piquette on holiday with his own family, to their cottage at Diamond Lake, is an attempt to alter the predicted course of Piquette's life. Inevitably Piquette is seen with mixed feelings by the young Vanessa. The story confirms the authenticity of Piquette's suffering and the strength of Vanessa's fascination with this untouchable girl who is finally perceived as the true aristocrat of Diamond Lake. The place is ironically later renamed Lake Wapakata, 'for it was felt that an Indian name would have a greater appeal to tourists.' (p. 126) 'The Loons' is an evocation of atmospheric stillness, a momentary glimpse of a way of life belonging to the past which has almost completely disappeared. Vanessa's holiday plans for Piquette quickly fade; her curiosity about Piquette's origins appears impertinent. 'It became increasingly apparent that, as an Indian, Piquette was a dead loss.' (pp. 120–21) The emotional content of the scene remains high, however: the death of Vanessa's father has been anticipated in the previous story, though he is still alive in this one. Vanessa is both drawn to and repelled by the crippled Métis child temporarily adopted by her family. The narrative induces a vision of a different order of things from that represented in the course of the story: not simply what it might have been like to grow up as Piquette Tonnerre instead of Vanessa MacLeod; but an intimation of the repressed history of the Métis and the way it still remains to be realized as a vital part of Vanessa's own background and cultural heritage.

The French writer Marthe Robert has a note on the subject of Canadian family romances which bears unexpected but striking relevance to Laurence's own remarks about claiming one's ancestors from the Métis. The note also helps to bring out the full psychological interest of the story discussed above. Robert's concern lies with the application of Freud's theory of the family romance to the development of the novel as a literary form. The author who gives occasion for her comments is Flaubert, who 'was not above following up an aristocratic connection in his ancestry', but who also revealed a significant pride in the supposed discovery of, translating Flaubert's words, a 'savage ancestress, a Natchez or an Iroquoi, I'm not sure which.' Marthe Robert's ensuing reflections on this point surely prompt certain questions about Laurence's attitude not only to the Métis but to the domestic atmosphere which forms the main environment of all the stories:

> Copious psychological observations stress the remarkable role played by Red Indians in North American and especially Canadian Family Romances where they presumably replace the historically non-existent aristocrat. The characteristics traditionally associated with them would favour such a substitution: the Red Indian is proud, noble, indomitable, generous and the rightful owner of the land. Compared to those who exterminate them the Indians can easily be seen as superior beings and thus replace Kings and Noble Fathers who occupy the most exalted position in the European Romance.[10]

As a generalization about the part played by Red Indians and aristocrats in Canadian history, this statement looks ill-informed. As an example of the kind of substitution of which romance is capable, it is more to the point. Robert's argument expressly concerns the displacement of autobiographical material into fiction and so it is appropriate to recall Laurence's description of the volume as the closest approach to autobiographical writing she made in fiction. The autobiographical impulse is there not only in the incidental detail of realistic presentation but even more decisively in the strong but strongly-controlled element of romance. 'The Loons', for example, is part of the imaginative design of A Bird in the House because the evocation of a lost world of Métis ancestors offsets the mediocrity of present reality. The opening recalls the moment at which the Métis, who might well have been considered the rightful owners of the land, 'entered their long silence' (p. 114). The stillness of Diamond Lake just survives at the time of Vanessa's childhood, though the close of the story retrospectively acknowledges that Piquette was 'the only one' (p. 127) to whom the former spirit of the place was perhaps still recognizable.

It is clear that for Laurence herself the wish to identify with these silent Métis ancestors is immensely strong. However to speak of an element of 'romance' in her fiction is not to deny her true concern with the actual history of the Métis, which is a commitment firmly resumed in her last novel, *The Diviners*. To be fully understood, the special appeal of the Métis cause must be measured against the kind of reality it opposes within the story: the view of the world embodied especially by Grandfather Connor, whom the author frankly described as based on her own maternal grandfather. The opposition between romance and reality provides access to the symbolic code of the narrative. The narrator, for example, recalls her juvenile disgust at the oft-recited 'epic' story of the day Grandfather Connor first arrived in Manawaka: 'Unfortunately he had not met up with any slit-eyed and treacherous Indians or any mad trappers, but only with ordinary farmers who had given him work shoeing their horses, for he was a blacksmith.' (p. 10) None of Vanessa's many childhood stories and daydreams, including the romantic misconception about Indians which affects her relationship with Piquette, allows her for a moment to triumph over given reality. But the writing clearly illustrates the psychological compulsion to question that reality. Of course the older narrator's telling of the story recognizes the compulsion.

Once the element of romance is given its proper emphasis, the other stories in *A Bird in the House* confirm Vanessa's inner struggle to find a richer meaning in the prosaic facts of her daily life. In 'The Mask of the Bear', the associations provided by her grandfather's coat generate an imaginative landscape remote from the atmosphere of the Brick House and illustrative of the metaphoric limits of a brick establishment (pp. 61–2):

> In my head I sometimes called him 'The Great Bear.' The name had many associations other than his coat and his surliness . . . In some unformulated way . . . I associated the secret name with Great Bear Lake, which I had seen only on maps and which I imagined to be a deep vastness of black water, lying somewhere very far beyond our known prairies of tamed fields and barbed-wire fences, somewhere in the regions of jagged rock and eternal ice, where human voices would be drawn into a cold and shadowed stillness without leaving even a trace of warmth.

Young Vanessa's imaginings are presented as a defensive strategy. They are both an attempt to relieve the atmosphere for herself and a recognition of the capacity for self-repression in adult life, of which her bear–grandfather is by no means the only example. We can appreciate the force of Laurence's acknowledgement of her own autobiographical investment in the book. Marthe Robert's argument entails the proposition that, by the very nature of the genre she employs, the novelist is dominated by a 'dialectic between the acceptance and the negation of reality'. This proves to be 'not only the source of endless original ideas' but also an indication of 'the actual pressure of creation' in the novelist's own circumstances.[11] Laurence, it may be remembered, is the novelist who at one time thought that she 'had written herself out of that prairie town' but later felt compelled to revise this statement, acknowledging that her mental horizons necessarily still centred on her conception of Manawaka: 'whatever I

am was shaped and formed in that sort of place and my way of seeing . . .
remains in some enduring way that of a small-town prairie person.'[12] The same
ambivalence is reflected in the persona of the narrator Vanessa MacLeod.

There is an unmistakeable power in Laurence's presentation of those
elements of romance which constitute the 'negation of reality' in her writing.
Vanessa's wayward inner development keeps this imaginative dimension of the
work constantly before the reader. She confesses her naive proprietory interest
in her cousin Chris, who comes from Shallow Creek: the place is still unknown
to her but her imagining of it illustrates again a psychological displacement of
the present order of things in the house, a continuing reaction against the only
kind of family life she knows (p. 134):

> His sisters – for Chris was the only boy – did not exist for me, not even
> as photographs, because I did not want them to exist. I wanted him to
> belong only here. Shallow Creek existed, though no longer filled with ice
> mountains in my mind but as some beckoning country beyond all ordi-
> nary considerations.

No doubt the foremost aspect of Laurence's writing is her deliberate insistence on common experience: her style is ultimately grounded on that. But her
realism incorporates a fierce rejection of the commonplace and a distrust of
what Robert Kroetsch calls 'certain traditional kinds of realism'. Vanessa
experiments in composing stories until she is finally ready to tell the story of
that childhood and its prolonged internal exile. It is clear that the story as
eventually told transgresses the cultural code which is supposed 'to set our
house in order' at the Brick House.

Kroetsch's theory of narrative proves to have a strong bearing on Laurence's
writing after all. The favourite strategy of contemporary Canadian writers,
Kroetsch has argued, is the breaking down of 'metanarratives'. This implies a
refusal to accept certain kinds of 'shared' or rather 'assumed' stories which had
come to acquire a privileged status in the community's cultural life.[13] Such
stories would include the epic of Grandfather Connor's arrival in Manawaka,
since that story represents a tradition which holds good for three generations
and has to be celebrated once more at the time of his death. In a significant
passage near the end of *A Bird in the House*, the narrator recalls how her
grandfather's death changed her perception of the story she herself had to tell
(p. 204):

> What funeral could my grandfather have been given except the one he
> got? The sombre hymns were sung, and he was sent to his Maker by the
> United Church minister, who spoke, as expected, of the fact that Timothy
> Connor had been one of Manawaka's pioneers . . . Then he had built his
> house. It had been the first brick house in Manawaka. Suddenly the
> minister's recounting of these familiar facts struck me as though I had
> never heard any of it before.

From the moment of his death, the inevitable 'recounting of these familiar facts' no longer represents the same threat to her. In her own narrative she is free to use the same facts and yet to refuse them the privileged interpretation which they had always seemed to carry.

Metanarratives are conveyed through recorded history as well as through literature and other sources. It is certain that Laurence considered herself more deeply engaged with the history of her own province than with any theory of fiction. The future of Manitoba itself has been subject in a peculiar way to rival views from its very beginnings. At the time of the Province's entry into the Dominion, a contemporary observer even suggested that:

> Manitoba has been to us on a small scale what Kansas was to the United States. It has been the battle-ground for our British and French elements with their respective religions, as Kansas was the battle-ground for Free Labour and Slavery. Ontario has played a part in contests there analogous to New England, Quebec to that of the southern states. The late government ... was, with respect to the Riel affair, in the position ... an American government, resting at once on Massachusetts and South Carolina, would have been with respect to Kansas.[14]

The origins of conflict are not forgotten in the small world of A Bird in the House. Grandfather MacLeod, for example, 'looked down on the Connors because they had come from famine Irish (although at least, thank God, Protestant)' (p. 63). Vanessa's last meeting with Piquette reveals to her the full extent to which her own experience of life in the same small town has been divided from that of the Métis girl, whose different future is already clearly marked in her face (p. 124):

> For the merest instant, then, I saw her. I really did see her for the first and only time in all the years we had both lived in the same town. Her defiant face, momentarily, became unguarded and unmasked, and in her eyes there was a terrifying hope.

The instant of recognition is realistically represented though the distance between them can never be bridged. Points where the narrative falters, where divisions suddenly become apparent within the generally unquestioned reality of everyday experience, continually recur. The stories which Vanessa has to tell contradict conventional wisdom even as they are moulded by its pressure. Conceived at once as a whole book and as a series of stories, A Bird in the House hesitates to assume the pattern of the oft-told tale, resists the formation of metanarrative.

There is a particular example of metanarrative which seems especially relevant to Laurence's fiction. This is 'the so-called nation-building approach to the Canadian past.'[15] Carl Berger outlines this approach in his examination of the career of the Canadian historian W. L. Morton, whose Manitoba: A History deeply impressed Laurence herself. Berger shows how Morton had felt compelled to challenge a certain type of reading of Canadian history which appeared to marginalize events in the West. The statement of 'the Laurentian theme', for example,

> rested on an economic interpretation of history and implied a homo-geneous view of Canadian experience; it relegated the history of the West to a peripheral question; and, above all, it was indifferent to the question of justice and equitable relations between the four sections and two races in Canada.[16]

Morton's profound opposition to such a view led him to wish for, in Berger's words, 'a history of the West written with such fidelity to the inner texture of local experience and so evocative of the sense of place that it would immedi-ately trigger a recognition in those who had been moulded by that tradition.'[17] There is no doubt of the close correspondence between Morton's history of Manitoba as it came to be written and Laurence's expanding conception of Manawaka. Having been moulded by the same tradition, Laurence was to appreciate the strong revision of Western history that Morton's approach implied. Morton had already praised the author of *The Stone Angel* in his book. She herself read *Manitoba: A History* during the summer in which she began writing *The Diviners*. But the coincidence of views between them goes back further. Commenting on this at the time of Morton's death, Laurence chose to emphasize their shared commitment to the idea of a multicultural society in Manitoba; and their realization that the 'many and varied histories' of its people must be strongly foregrounded: 'What I share, most of all, with Morton is the sense of my *place*, the prairies, and of my *people* (meaning all prairie peoples), within the context of their many and varied histories, and the desire to make all these things come alive in the reader's mind.'[18] Neither the historian nor the novelist was satisfied with previously assumed stories of provincial life.

Morton developed an even stronger emphasis in the second edition of his work. He envisaged a potentially 'prosperous, rational, humane and vivid society' which must be achieved by overcoming 'the mediocrity of survival as it was and had been'.[19] The community history which the stories of *A Bird in the House* relate is the imaginative record of an insider to that struggle during a critical period. The household is touched by the general crises of the period, as they affected Manitoba. The Battle of the Somme is part of living memory to Vanessa's father, though Vanessa herself is embarrassed by the annual parade of veterans; the Battle of Britain and the raid on Dieppe are recent events as the narrative closes. The question forced from Edna near the opening of the book has by then accumulated more significance for Vanessa herself: ' "Won't this damn Depression ever be over? I can see myself staying on and on here in this house – ." ' (p. 14) Vanessa's stories suggest in domestic detail how the general pressure of the times is transmitted locally into 'the mediocrity of survival'. But the text as written can never be reconciled with that prospect as the complete reality. Laurence herself can be seen as a committed but realist, but deeply opposed to a form of realism which would appear to take for granted the conditions it describes. Her semi-autobiographical fiction takes so little for granted that it represents one of the strongest revisions of Western experience in contemporary Canadian writing.

### Notes

References are made to the New Canadian Library edition of *A Bird in the House*; page numbers are given in the text of the essay.
 1  The author would like to thank Macmillan for permission to use material previously published as 'The Realism of Lawrence's Semi-autobiographical Fiction' in *Critical Approaches to Margaret Laurence*, 1990.
 2  David Lodge, *The Modes of Modern Writing*, London, Edward Arnold, 1983, p. 52.
 3  George Woodcock (ed.), *A Place to Stand On: Essays by and about Margaret Laurence*, Edmonton, NeWest Press, 1983, p. 156.
 4  Woodcock, p. 208.
 5  Woodcock, p. 4.
 6  'Conversation with Margaret Laurence', in *A Place to Stand On*, pp. 46–55.
 7  Ibid.
 8  Woodcock, p. 157.
 9  Woodcock, p. 275.
10  Marthe Robert, *Origins of the Novel*, trans. Sacha Rabinovitch, Brighton, The Harvester Press, 1980, p. 235.
11  Robert, p. 144.
12  Woodcock, p. 19.
13  Robert Kroetsch, 'Disunity as Unity: A Canadian Strategy', in Colin Nicholson and Peter Easingwood (eds), *Canadian Story and History 1885–1985*, Edinburgh, Centre of Canadian Studies, 1986, pp. 1–11.
14  See Doug Owram, *Promise of Eden: The Canadian Expansionist Movement and the Idea of the West 1856–1900*, Toronto, University of Toronto Press, 1980, pp. 99–100.
15  Carl Berger, *The Writing of Canadian History*, Toronto, Oxford University Press, 1976, p. 256.
16  Berger, p. 241.
17  Berger, p. 246.
18  Margaret Laurence, 'W. L. Morton: a personal tribute', *Journal of Canadian Studies*, 15:4 1981, p. 134.
19  W. L. Morton, *Manitoba: A History*, 2nd ed. Toronto, University of Toronto Press, 1967, p. 502.

# 3

# The Tuning of Memory: Alistair MacLeod's Short Fiction[1]

**Colin Nicholson**

On 25 February 1986, in Edinburgh, Paul Ricoeur delivered as the fifth of his Gifford Lectures *On Selfhood: The Question of Personal Identity*, a paper which he called 'Narrative identity'. The lecture considered the temporal dimensions of the self, and although my own antennae were attuned in particular ways by the work I had been doing on Alistair MacLeod's short narratives, I was none the less surprised at the ways in which the lecture seemed to address itself directly and in some detail to the concerns of MacLeod's fiction. 'What is it', Ricoeur asked, 'that assures the identity of the self throughout the history that unfolds between birth and death? How can the permanence and change of the personality be reconciled?' He went on to suggest that within the framework of language, the temporal dimension of life is narrative; a live history thereby becomes a narrative history. By identifying itself with what Ricoeur termed the figuration of character, the self acquires a concrete identity, refigured by the mediation of narrative: a narrative identity. Both the autobiographical mode of many of MacLeod's short stories and their insistent seeking out of a present tense registration for affective memory give point and shade and definition to Ricoeur's speculations. MacLeod constructs a deeply historicized discourse in which self and other endlessly merge, diverge and recombine.

Reviewing the seven stories which comprise MacLeod's first collection, *The Lost Salt Gift of Blood*[2], Matt Cohen remarked,

> these people earn their living, and it is not a very good one, in semi-suicidal conditions: mines filled with rats, dampness, the possibility of collapse or explosion; or fishing in waters which have become polluted or

fished-out with the passing of time. And so the young people dream of escape, while their parents and grandparents hope they will stay on – to support them – but also hope they will leave – to find an easier life for themselves . . .'[3]

It is an acute summary, and one which takes us back to Ricoeur and forward to the techniques which MacLeod develops to give experiential voice to the historical environment and regional contours of his native Nova Scotia. We can trace in this slender volume the processes of growing up in and away from a delimiting and economically determined childhood. But they are determinations which also lend substance to self-definition. As the stories compose a meditation upon time and identity, lines from Eliot's *Four Quartets* provide a persuasive gloss:

> Home is where one starts from. As we grow older
> The world becomes stranger, the pattern more complicated
> Of dead and living. Not the intense moment
> Isolated, with no before and after,
> But a lifetime burning in every moment
> And not the lifetime of one man only
> But of old stones that cannot be deciphered.[4]
>
> 'East Coker', V

We will watch the burden of those lines recur, but meanwhile we can note that one of the seeming constancies in the changing emotional landscape of these stories is a use of the child as a focal point for narrative event. The first, 'In the Fall', narrated by James, a boy of almost fourteen, charts the violent eruption of difference into a hitherto ordered and orderly, if harsh, existence when necessity demands the selling of a loved but economically burdensome and sickly horse. Rude intrusions of monetary actuality mark a decisive shift out of childhood as memory and desire now begin to mix differently (p. 25):

> And I think I begin to understand for the first time how difficult and perhaps how fearful it is to be an adult and I am suddenly and selfishly afraid not only for myself now but for what it seems I am to be.

Typical of MacLeod's use of grammatical precision,[5] the boy's growing sense of self-awareness projects itself as a wider movement in the shift from I to you as the narrator describes his difficult way back into the house. Then, referring to his ten-year-old brother, the final sentence gestures ambiguously towards a future promise. 'I think I will try to find David, that perhaps he may understand' (p. 30).

'The Vastness of the Dark' figures an eighteen year old discovering that mere physical journeying out from childhood environs brings no guarantee of release or escape. Memories of a coal-mining family history and his own extra-marital conception within it are the mental and emotional freight he must always carry with him. In 'The Return' a ten year old is the focalizing agent in an uneasy revisiting of his father's family origins. And eighteen, too, is the age of the conscience-stricken, pool-playing schoolboy, presented in the third person, in 'The Golden Gift of Grey'. Learning that parental habits and beliefs are more resilient than he had anticipated, he learns also that an ambiguous grey offers relaxation from a tight parental coding of moral black and white which his own preferred experience is already guiltily destabilizing. While the remaining three stories centre on first person adult narration, in each case a past is continually recoiling. Plots construct emotional returns to earlier events whose effects resonate within and thereby structure an unsettled and unsettling present. In these tales the child is father of the man in calculated and disturbing ways.

In the much anthologized story 'The Boat', this trajectory of feeling produces a narrative which offers itself as a paradigm of MacLeod's favoured techniques. Already resonating with the possibility that this child may also have grown to become author of the father's death as well as his textual reincarnation, the disconcerting now in which the narrative voice awakens to begin its story sets a contextual immediacy for the shaping operations of a preterite existence which everywhere disrupts, infiltrates and defines the parameters of narrative contemporaneity. This is a presented voice so thoroughly imbued by past relationships that it appears inseparable from the recalled experience to which it gives utterance. Memory is everywhere pre-text, as the I which speaks in the now of our reading brings us to participant awareness of a complex, shared formation (p. 129):

> There are times even now, when I awake at four o'clock in the morning with the terrible fear that I have overslept; when I imagine that my father is waiting for me in the room below the darkened stairs or that the shore-bound men are tossing pebbles against my window while blowing their hands and stomping their feet impatiently on the frozen steadfast earth. There are times when I am half out of bed and fumbling for socks and mumbling for words before I realize that I am foolishly alone, that no one waits at the base of the stairs and no boat rides restlessly in the waters by the pier.

This image of the fishermen at his window is to surface on two subsequent occasions: the first when the narrator recalls that his father 'would make no attempt to wake me himself' (p. 146), the last when he imagines his now isolated mother still listening to (p. 150)

> The rubber boots of the men scrunch upon the gravel as they pass beside her house on their way down to the wharf. And she knows that the footsteps never stop, because no man goes from her house, and she alone of all the Lynns has neither son nor son-in-law that walks towards the boat that will take him to the sea. And it is not an easy thing to know that your mother looks upon the sea with love and on you with bitterness because the one has been so constant and the other so untrue.

'The Boat''s second paragraph continues to register the present of the remembering adult, noticing 'the grey corpses of the overflowing ashtray beside my bed' (p. 129). This too prescribes a later memory, from earlier days, of his father's bedside table: 'a deck of cigarette papers and an overflowing ashtray cluttered its surface' (p. 134). The word overflowing connects remembered images, and 'surface' in the second, further prefigures the father's dying. As for Eliot's persona, so for our narrator:

> It seems, as one becomes older
> That the past has another pattern, and ceases to be a mere sequence –
> Or even development
>
> 'The Dry Salvages', II, p. 186

The comforting attempt by our narrator to separate himself from these initial footfalls in the memory – 'they are only shadows and echoes, the animals a child's hands make on the wall by lamplight, and the voices from the rain barrel; the cuttings from an old movie made in the black and white of long ago' (p. 130) – is deconstructed by the very discourse in which the attempt is embedded. As the phrase 'long ago' leads, in the following paragraph, into the story's first and momentary deployment of the past tense, we discover that this past will not be so easily located in a fixed and knowable time and space. The opening act of waking up leads on now to a narrative reconstruction of the boy's dawning consciousness.

His first memory of his father is sensuous; aromatic and tactile, whereas 'my earliest recollection of my mother is of being alone with her in the mornings while my father was away in the boat' (p. 131). Moreover, the boat is named Jenny Lynn, his mother's maiden name, 'as another link in the chain of tradition' (p. 132), and that image itself links forward to 'the bracelets of brass chain which [my father] wore to protect his wrists from chafing' (p. 141). So a father's prior entrapment in a life of work to which he is not even bodily suited is signalled by a recurrence of the same image. 'The chafe-preventing bracelets of brass linked chain that all the men wore about their wrists in early spring were his the full season' (p. 146). With the story's concluding image, the father's corpse crumbling in the hands of our remembering narrator, an image which returns us to the nightmarish beginning, we see this lasting enchainment. 'There was not much left of my father, physically, as he lay there with the brass chains on his wrist and the seaweed in his hair' (p. 151). In its mental transfigurations, of course, the dead father always already haunts the narrative. The structure of the plot is the patterning of recall, and this sense of an ending forms a continuing present in which there is no terminal situation. Eliot again seems relevant to the reader's encounter, where

> The end of all our exploring
> Will be to arrive where we started
> And know the place for the first time.
>
> 'Little Gidding', V, p. 197

With perhaps this qualification: that in Alistair MacLeod's fiction there seems to be no identifiable first time, and all narrative unfoldings are themselves preterite, pre-scribings of sequences which are always already pre-texts for the on going act of imaginative memory.

From his mother the boy learns more than is immediately apparent (p. 131).

> When my father returned about noon, she would ask, 'Well, how did things go in the boat today?' It was the first question I remember asking: 'Well, how did things go in the boat today?' 'Well, how did things go in the boat today?'

As one of the text's many unspoken reverberations, the reader is left to realize who asked the question on the father's last day, and how, and by whom it was and continues to be answered. These silent registrations of the text are voluble. But the mother asks another question, this time in hostile tones, of the tourist visitors to Nova Scotia from a world beyond her literal horizons; tourists who take her daughters away, to a world which thus threatens her hard earned security (p. 137):

> 'Who are these people anyway?' she would ask, tossing back her dark hair, 'and what do they, though they go about with their cameras for a hundred years, know about the way it is here, and what do they care about me and mine, and why should I care about them?'

It is a question which the narrative persona turns back upon his own people, exploring his and their motivations and desires. In the telling of his tale he opens his and their lives and ambitions to the wider world of experience in which the boy, his sisters and his father have either sought to participate or have joined.

But that joining is also a separation, and in the world of these stories it becomes apparent that nothing can be left behind. Language is left to achieve whatever duplicitous constancies it may. When, in 'The Boat', the boy who has since become a university lecturer promises his father to 'remain with him as long as he lived and [they] would fish the sea together', his father 'only smiled through the cigarette smoke that wreathed his bed and replied, "I hope you will remember what you've said" ' (p. 147). During that last fateful fishing season the boy's mother had said ' "you have given added years to his life" ' (p. 148). These things linger in the recall of one who must go on living with the very real possibility that his father's death by drowning was a wilful act to accomplish the boy's release from a world of work which the father experienced as relentless and unsatisfying. Again, the boy's hopeless attempt in a stormy sea to mount a rescue operation for his drowned father by turning the boat 'in a wide and stupid circle' (p. 149) conjures, in tragic reprise, his father's manoeuvre during the infant boy's first sailing in a calm enclosure – 'in the harbour we made our little circle and returned' (p. 131).

What might register as random contingency in existential encounter, exhibits iterative structure in recall. Knowing this, the narrator must accept opposing senses: of uncertainty in lived experience and patterned inevitability in narrative reconstruction. For 'The Boat' itself encodes a narrative response, if you like an answerable discourse, to the father's voice which had sung 'the wild and haunting Gaelic war songs of those spattered highland ancestors he had never seen' (p. 140). That voice had in turn wrought transforming effects for the retaining narrative consciousness: 'when his voice ceased, the savage melancholy of three hundred years seemed to hang over the peaceful harbour' (p. 140). The melancholy survives in the son's narration.

Such bardic intimations of mortality figure also in the stories of MacLeod's second collection, called *As Birds Bring Forth the Sun*.[6] Its opening story, 'The Closing Down of Summer', seems in many ways to articulate, directly and alternatively, with 'The Boat'. Spoken this time by a miner called MacKinnon, leader of what he proudly boasts is 'perhaps the best crew of shaft and development miners in the world' (p. 12), it brings into different focus aspects of emotional self-definition which play beneath the surface of the earlier story. Characterized again by a narrative commitment to the present tense, 'The Closing Down of Summer' excavates modes of constancy against which autobiographical change might be measured.

The youth in 'The Boat', who does what his father desires but cannot accomplish, leaving fishing for a university education, finds intertextual response in a young man who leaves university after only one year 'spent mainly as an athlete and as a casual reader of English literature' (p. 29), to become the miner he now is. As in 'The Boat', encounters with literary texts prove to be sharply double edged pleasures. In that story, the young boy read *Great Expectations* and discussed *David Copperfield* with his father, provoking self-reflexive comparisons between MacLeod's narrator and those of Dickens. In 'The Boat', too, the choice of 'useless books over the parents that gave him life' (p. 144) leaves our narrator with the forlorn wish 'that the two things I loved so dearly did not exclude each other in a manner that was so blunt and too clear' (p. 145). He remains troubled by the knowledge that 'the grounds my father fished were those his father fished before him and there were others before and before and before' (p. 149), and that to those who remain behind, those fishing grounds 'are sacred and they think they wait for me' (p. 150).

Differently, and then similarly, in 'The Closing Down of Summer', university is soon abandoned by a narrator impressed 'by the fact that I was from a mining family that has given itself for generations to the darkened earth' (p. 29):

I was aware of the ultimate irony of my choice. Aware of how contradictory it seemed that someone who was bothered by confinement should choose to spend his working days in the most confined of spaces. Yet the difference seems to be that when we work we are never still. Never merely entombed like the prisoner in the passive darkness of his solitary confinement. For we are always expanding the perimeters of our seeming incarceration. We are always moving downward or inward or forward or in the driving of our raises even upward.

Referring to the comparatively banal existence of his estranged wife's entrapment in the conventional world of commodity fetishism, MacKinnon says (p. 23)

> she has perhaps gone as deeply into that life as I have into the life of the shafts, seeming to tunnel ever downward and outward through unknown depths and distances and to become lost and separated and unavailable for communication . . . Perhaps we are but becoming our previous generation.

This subterranean metaphor undergoes further mutation when MacKinnon ponders the possible significations of a mining gang travelling the world, 'liberating resources' (p. 30) and then moving on, leaving the mines to be developed by other workers underground, producing the profits from which social structures are built. The societies are in turn subjected to all kinds of political transformations, through all of which 'Renco Development on Bay Street' will wait for the miners 'who would find such booty' (p. 31).

If the act of mining develops metaphorically into a narrative enigma, the words 'constant' and 'constancy' compose an iterative figuration as lexical icons. The topography of textuality itself becomes the subject of narrating memory's excavations. Inscriptions of mortality recur; durable on tombstones, 'reading the dates of our brothers and uncles and cousins' (p. 17), and in 'the yellow telegram . . . permanent in the starkness of its message' (p. 19), or else transiently with the telephone call which 'seems somehow to fade with the passing of time' (p. 19) yet which survives in memory. All of these become texts to be read, signs to be deciphered. MacKinnon recognizes that he is looking for 'patterns older than memory' (p. 21) and striving simultaneously for an articulate equivalence to the eloquent and satisfying physicality of working in the mines. Facing the frequency of violent deaths in mineshafts the world over, it may seem natural that MacKinnon's miners 'have perhaps gone back to the Gaelic songs because they are so constant and unchanging and speak to us as the privately familiar' (p. 24). But even this comes to symbolize an entombed activity, 'lacking in communication' (p. 24). Their professional appearances as MacKinnon's Miners' Chorus eventually become (p. 24)

> as lonely and irrelevant as it was meaningless. It was as if we were parodies of ourselves, standing in rows, wearing our miners' gear, or being asked to shave and wear suits, being plied with rum while waiting for our turn on the program, only then to mouth our songs to batteries of tape recorders and to people who did not understand them.

MacKinnon tries to read meaning in the art of Zulu dancing which he had seen in the Africa to which he is about to return, and does indeed feel some kinship with it. But 'their dancing', he is forced to concede, 'speaks a language whose true meaning will elude me forever. I will never grasp the full impact of the subtleties and nuances that are spoken by the small head gesture or the flashing fleck of muscle' (p. 25). He sees, though, connections between his watching the Zulus and his miners singing to a dwindling band of comprehending listeners. The sense of narrative foreboding which pervades our text seems to owe as much to MacKinnon's keen perception that the culture from which he originates is itself fading as it does to any sense of impending personal jeopardy. And his disgruntlement at the inefficacy of language leads to this, where the limits of his words are felt as the limit of his world: 'We have sentenced ourselves to enclosures so that we might feel the giddy joy of breaking through. Always hopeful of breaking through though we know we will never break free' (p. 30). The contending possibilities of Gaelic and of English as surviving systems of communication are compared with the lot of a French–Canadian mining gang who 'will not go to Africa for Renco Development because they are imprisoned in the depths of their language' (p. 31).

As they leave the beach on which they have been 'lying now in the ember of summer's heat and in the stillness of its time' (p. 16), another sign of evanescence is read upon the sand (p. 33).

> Our footprints of brief moments before already have been washed away. There remains no evidence that we have ever been. It is as if we have never lain, nor ever walked nor ever thought what thoughts we had. We leave no art or mark behind. The sea has washed its sand slate clean.

And given the density of Gaelic reference in this and other stories, and their signifying function as a historic system of registration, it becomes difficult not to be aware of a further referential curve. Vanishing traces on a shoreline here conjure associations with those clearances elsewhere, equally determined by the economic motivations of others, when people were herded to the sea's edge and translated from highlands and islands on the western fringe of Europe to this easternmost island landfall on Canada's Atlantic coast. A gathering sense of peripheral impermanence seems in both cases to be an appropriate structure of feeling. Certainly there is a painful contour in these stories of dispossession and emotional deracination. Gracefully transformed in a memorably written present, it aches none the less.

MacLeod's art ensures his own compromised survival. Linguistic and cultural continuity is an autobiographical problematic for the author himself. He belongs to the first generation of Cape Bretoners not to be brought up as native speakers of Gaelic. His literary accomplishment in giving line and form to the people of Nova Scotia is disconcerted by the fact that his mastery of English literary discourse itself marks a process of change and slippage from historic origins. So it is hardly surprising that the echoing resonances which characterize his writing prevent any easy assimilation into the present which his stories adumbrate. At the end of 'The Closing Down of Summer' the imbrication of time past and time present achieves a different kind of intertextual configuration and the nature of textuality is again foregrounded:

> More than a quarter of a century ago in my single year at university, I stumbled across an anonymous lyric from the fifteenth century. Last night while packing my clothes, I encountered it again, this time in the literature text of my eldest daughter. The book was very different from the one I had so casually used, as different perhaps as is my daughter from me. Yet the lyric was exactly the same. It had not changed at all. It comes to me now in this speeding car as the Gaelic choruses rise around me. I do not particularly welcome it or want it and indeed I had almost forgotten it. Yet it enters now regardless of my wants or wishes, much as one might see out of the corner of the eye an old acquaintance one has no wish to see at all. It comes again unbidden and unexpected and imperfectly remembered. It seems borne up by the mounting, surging Gaelic voices like the flecked white foam on the surge of the towering, breaking wave. Different yet similar, and similar yet different, and in its time unable to deny:

> I wend to death, Knight stith in stour;
> Through fight in field I won the flower;
> No fights me taught the death to quell –
> I wend to death, sooth I you tell.
> I wend to death, a king iwis;
> What helpes honour or worlde's bliss?
> Death is to man the final way –
> I wende to be clad in clay.

Across five hundred years an elegizing lyric speaks its own perception of present ending. But it, too, is textually complicated. The source for these verses is a Latin poem in thirty-four distiches printed from a thirteenth-century manuscript.[6] Not only is literary textuality thus historicized, its mode of existence is further compromised in the now of MacKinnon's remembrance. When he read the lines in his daughter's literature text, 'the lyric was exactly the same. It had not changed at all' from the time he first encountered it. But as it returns again, 'unbidden and unexpected and imperfectly remembered', it changes in crucial respects. First written on scrolls, this present tense lyric was composed in four quatrains. In a deconstructive turn our narrator ruptures the enclosure of this text by reproducing only two quatrains from the original. He then, in the uncertain recuperation of his memory inserts the word 'final' where the original produced 'kynde':

> Death is to man the kynde way
> I wende to be clad in clay

'Kynde' means natural, and signifies an acceptance very different from MacKinnon's own. The 'patterns older than memory' for which he searches are traced in the discourse which presents him. But it is a kind of discourse which resists closure. No longer positing the consolation of permanence, the literary text offers, rather, the discursive possibility of intertextual relationships: relationships which demonstrably modulate with changing time and circumstance. There is no still point in its turning world. In Alistair MacLeod's writing, our past is recuperated in a continuous present: uncertain, jeopardized even, but open still, and still possible.

### Notes

1 First appeared in RANAM (Recherches Anglaises et Americaines), 20, 1987, pp. 85–93.
2 Alistair MacLeod, *The Lost Salt Gift of Blood*, Toronto, McClelland and Stewart, 1976. Subsequent citations are given parenthetically in the text.
3 Matt Cohen, *Edmonton Journal*, 6 March 1976.
4 T.S. Eliot, *Four Quartets*, in *The Complete Poems and Plays of T.S. Eliot*, London, Faber and Faber, 1969, p. 182. Subsequent citations are given parenthetically in the text.
5 Simone Vauthier gives a detailed account of this precision in her analysis of a single story, 'Notes sur l'emploi du present dans "The Road to Rankin's Point" d'Alistair MacLeod,' in *RANAM*, 14, 1983, pp. 143–58.
6 Alistair MacLeod, *As Birds Bring Forth the Sun and Other Stories*, Toronto, McClelland and Stewart, 1986. Subsequent citations are given parenthetically in the text.
7 Carleton Brown, (ed.), *Lyrics of the Fifteenth Century*, Oxford, Oxford University Press, 1939, pp. 248–9, and note 157, p. 340.

# 4

# 'Historical Relations': Modes of Discourse in Michael Ondaatje's *Running in the Family*

## John A. Thieme

Few writers stand at the confluence of as many cultures as Michael Ondaatje. While his name is Dutch in origin, he comes from a mixed Sri Lankan background, was educated in England and, while now living in Canada, is well known for his writing about American mythologies in such books at *The Collected Works of Billy the Kid* (1970) and *Coming Through Slaughter* (1976). Despite this Ondaatje's work is typically Canadian in many of its preoccupations. His concern to explore the past and how cultural mythologies are formed, his postmodernist investigations of language and form and his attempts to break down generic barriers in texts which mix various modes of prose and poetry with visual and documentary material all make him one of the most typically Canadian writers of the contemporary period. Thus a text like *The Collected Works of Billy the Kid* proves, despite its American subject matter, to have much in common with the writing of Canadians like Robert Kroetsch, George Bowering, B.P. Nichol – about whom Ondaatje has made a film[1] – and Bill Bissett, all of whom have collapsed the boundaries between discourses in their attempts not only to deconstruct received versions of language and history, but also to reconstruct them in alternative paradigms.

In this sense *Running in the Family* (1982), while ostensibly a personal travel journal in which the writer attempts to rediscover his Sri Lankan roots, is also a quintessentially Canadian text, demonstrating a concern with how notions of personal and cultural identity are formed through language. And it shares the preoccupation with origins, and specifically with genealogy, that characterizes much of the best contemporary Canadian fiction, such as Margaret Atwood's *Surfacing* (1972), Margaret Laurence's *The Diviners* (1974), Robert

Kroetsch's *Badlands* (1975) and Jack Hodgin's *The Invention of the World* (1977).[2]

The personal odyssey on which the writer sets out in *Running in the Family* is both a public and a private quest: an exploration of the past of Sri Lanka as well as an investigation into his own personal past. It is at the same time a textual journey, in which numerous modes of discourse are juxtaposed within the dominant pattern of a discontinuous narrative to suggest the arbitrariness of generic classification and the limitations of fixed-form narrative for something as complex as trying to provide an account of 'Historical Relations' (the title of one of the narrative's many sections).[3] Indeed this very phrase encapsulates much of the elusiveness of the genealogical quest being undertaken in the work. The narrator investigates his own personal history as well as the construction of notions of Sri Lankan ancestry; at the same time his text may be seen as dramatizing the problem of *relating* history, whether personal or public, and the difficulty of establishing *relationships* between areas of history. The work very clearly locates itself within a postmodernist tradition, resisting unitary classification, closure and essentialist definitions of personality and the past, and suggesting that both individual and national identities are formed through a series of random, and frequently bizarre, accretions. Towards the end there is a vivid image of a disintegrating book (p. 189):

> In the bathroom ants had attacked the novel thrown on the floor by the commode. A whole battalion was carrying one page away from its source, carrying the intimate print as if rolling a tablet away from him. He knelt down on the red tile slowly, not wishing to disturb their work. It was page 189. He had not got that far in the book yet but he surrendered it to them . . .

The passage conveys the distinct sense that the text itself is disintegrating at this point, particularly since the page on which it comes is in fact 'p. 189'. But this is only typical of the whole of *Running in the Family*. Earlier there has been a similar passage in which silverfish are seen as destroying the photographs in family albums, photographs which are a paradigm of the kind of genealogical evidence that the text is investigating (pp. 135–6):

> the silverfish slid into steamer trunks and photograph albums – eating their way through portraits and wedding pictures. What images of family life they consumed in their minute jaws and took into their bodies no thicker than the pages they ate.

And for much of the time one does not so much have the sense of a deconstructed text as of one which foregrounds the problem of arriving at any kind of construction at all.

If initially such a passage seems to work in much the same way as a similar passage in Jean Rhys's *Wide Sargasso Sea* (1966), in which Rochester – a man much metamorphosed from the Byronic hero of *Jane Eyre* on whom he is based – discovers a number of Romantic books decaying in the tropical ambience of the Dominican house where he is staying,[4] in fact the implications of the decaying or consumed texts are arguably very different. In *Wide Sargasso Sea* the decay seems to represent the fate of English Romanticism in the tropics, a predicament commented on by Huxley in his essay 'Wordsworth in the Tropics',[5] and one which is highly relevant in this context, both in terms of what is happening to Rochester and what is happening to the English Romantic text, *Jane Eyre*, as it is reworked and subverted by the tropical text, *Wide Sargasso Sea*, written, metaphorically at least, from the other side of the cultural divide suggested by the novel's title. In *Running in the Family* the image functions less as an index of cultural difference and more as a commentary on the fugitive nature of past experiences and the impossibility of constructing a definitive version in discourse. Just before the very end the book openly acknowledges its incompleteness in a passage in which the writer directly addresses his father (p. 201) – representative of the patriarchal aspect of tradition and the society from which he issues:[6]

> 'You must get this book right', my brother tells me, 'You can only write it once.' But the book again is incomplete. In the end all your children move among the scattered acts and memories with no more clues. Not that we ever thought we would be able to fully understand you. Love is often enough, towards your stadium of small things . . .

His father, who has now become the central figure in the exploration of ancestry and the past, defies total comprehension. In a suggestive metafictive reference, which foregrounds the relationship between the narrator's endeavour to understand his father and the reading process itself, he is seen as like 'one of those books we long to read whose pages remain uncut' (p. 200). Like the text itself he has become an insoluble detective story: there are not enough clues to solve the mystery, though this does not preclude the possibility of delicately observed minimalist insights into the operation of language and the ways in which notions of identity are constructed; nor does it negate the kind of loving homage, which emerges in these final pages, pages which suggest the kind of relationship between love and discourse which has been charted by critics like Roland Barthes.[7]

Among the many modes of discourse in *Running in the Family* there are a variety of prose narratives, which appear to move between the factual and the fictive, often without providing any clear demarcation line. In a section of 'Acknowledgments', located not at the beginning but at the very end of the work, Ondaatje confesses (p. 206):

> While all these names may give an air of authenticity, I must confess that the book is not a history but a portrait or 'gesture'. And if those listed above disapprove of the fictional air I apologize and can only say that in Sri Lanka a well-told lie is worth a thousand facts.

There is no doubt that the book provides some kind of account of the narrator's family past, but its demonstration of the inevitably piecemeal and fragmentary quality of the attempt at genealogical reclamation makes it primarily a text about the problematics of constructing a discourse of the past; and some sections, such as the narrative of the death of his grandmother Lalla in a flood and a passage about his father's last days, can only be speculation of an essentially fictive kind on the author's part.

Much of his material has come to him from oral storytelling sources. Sometimes the oral is presented in the form of dialogues, some of which are attributed to specific speakers, others of which are left anonymous (while raising the strong suspicion that the speakers are the writers' siblings or aunts, who prove to be his most important sources of information about the past) and have the effect of reinforcing the assertion, again made in the Acknowledgement at the end, that 'A literary work is a communal act' (p. 205). This oral storytelling has a humorous anecdotal quality about it that provides the text with one of its most distinctive stylistic qualities. Ondaatje identity is presented as comic, bizarre and outrageous; his family emerge as a collection of eccentrics, who appear to be compulsively committed to excess. The extent to which such representation is a product of the storytellers' mediating voices is hard to gauge. The possibility that oral accounts can involve exaggeration is explicitly suggested at one point (p. 138) and many readers will have the suspicion that the comic excesses that characterize the narrator's family throughout may owe more than a little to the memories of those who relate the tales of outrageous behaviour in the past and their mode of formulating their anecdotes. Late on in the work a more specific origin for the hyperbolical mode of comic reportage emerges in a passage which characterizes the particular quality of Ondaatje's mother's storytelling (p. 169):

> She belonged to a type of Ceylonese family whose women would take the minutest reaction from another and blow it up into a tremendously exciting tale, then later use it as an example of someone's strain of character. If anything kept their generation alive it was this recording by exaggeration. Ordinary tennis matches would be mythologized to the extent that one player was so drunk that he almost died on the court. An individual would be eternally remembered for one small act that in five years had become so magnified he was just a footnote below it.

Such a manner lies at the heart of many of the portraits that make up the family album of *Running in the Family* itself. Perhaps this is because of the nature of the various voices that inform the babel of the text: those parts which emanate from the narrator's aunts and from family friends of his mother's generation can very reasonably be expected to engage in this kind of utterance, since they come from the same stock, the same 'type of Ceylonese family'. But one has the sense that the narrative's indebtedness to such a mode goes beyond simply reflecting the voices of some of those whose accounts have fed into the text. And again this suspicion is confirmed towards the end, when the author realizes that his own penchant for telling tall stories, and for dramatization more generally, derives, not from his father, who despite his 'temporary manic public behaviour' (p. 168) is essentially secretive, but from his histrionic mother. She it is, one may argue, who is the single most important presence behind his producing 'not a history but a portrait or "gesture" '.

Among the many other modes of discourse employed in *Running in the Family* are photographs, journal entries, quotations and poems. The juxtaposition of modes, without any one being privileged over any other, again has the effect of drawing attention to the impossibility of producing an absolutist history, whether personal or public. Many of the work's short sections are themselves like the snapshots that punctuate the text; they offer single windows on to the past, which give minimalist insights; but since they are left essentially unrelated to other sections – there is little sense of linear movement in *Running in the Family* – a clear historical pattern fails to emerge.

The narrator's stance is essentially ambivalent: he presents himself as both insider and outsider; as both *Karapotha* (his niece's term for 'foreigner', from 'the beetles with white spots who never grew ancient here' (p. 80) and returned 'prodigal'. And he is a mixture of insider and outsider in another sense: as both an onlooker and participant in the action he describes. Most of the time his role is that of a witness or auditor. He offers visual witness, mediated (except in the case of the photographs that are reproduced in the text) through language, recording evidence gleaned from a variety of written sources, including old newspapers, commentaries on Ceylon by visiting 'Karapothas' and brass plagues on church walls, as well as providing responses to what he sees in the present with his own eyes. And as an auditor he receives and records the many oral accounts of the past of his family and their associates. Sometimes in such narratives, for example when his brother and sisters tell him about his father (pp. 173–8), there is a very strong sense that the recipient of the information is the pivotal point of the action and in this particular section this is expressed lexically by the frequent use of the second-person pronoun and the section's being entitled 'Dialogues', even though the format is ostensibly that of a series of monologues. So the stress here is on the supposedly passive recipient as the protagonist, and rightly so since, as the reader, selector and orderer of the various elements that make up the text, he is its key figure, even when his own narrative voice is suspended.

Elsewhere his role is less akin to that of reader and closer to the more conventional notion of the author as creator. Occasionally his own remembrance of things past forms part of the evidence on which the textual evidence is based. At other times his response to the present of Sri Lanka and his attempt to relate this to memories of his tropical childhood become key ingredients. Beyond this the particular quality of his prose – lyrical, evocative and at times highly poetic – imposes a particular filter on the material. It is a filter which, without exactly sentimentalizing, initially seems to turn the past rose-coloured. This is particularly the case in a section entitled 'A Fine Romance', which locates his parents and their generation as products of the 1920s and suggests that, at least for those of their social class, the hallmark of life in the Ceylon of the Roaring Twenties was the same kind of careless insouciance as characterized the decade elsewhere. In passages like the following Ondaatje writes a heightened, condensed prose that is strongly redolent of the most famous chronicler of the Jazz Age (pp. 40–1):[8]

> The gardens were full of cypress, rhododendrons, fox-gloves, arumlilies and sweet pea; and people like the van Langenbergs, the Vernon Dickmans, the Henry de Mels and the Philip Ondaatjes were there. There were casual tragedies. Lucas Cantley's wife Jessica almost died after being shot by an unknown assailant while playing croquet with my grandfather. They found 113 pellets in her. 'And poor Wilfred Batholomeusz who had large teeth was killed while out hunting when one of his companions mistook him for a wild boar.'
>
> During the month of May the circus came to Nuwara Eliya. Once, when the circus lights failed, Major Robinson drove the fire engine into the tent and focused the headlights on the trapeze artist, who had no intention of continuing and sat there straddling his trapeze. At one of these touring circuses my Aunt Christie (then only twenty-five) stood up and volunteered to have an apple shot off her head by 'a total stranger in the circus profession'. That night T.W. Roberts was bitten in the leg by a dog while he danced with her. Later the dog was discovered to be rabid, but as T.W. had left for England nobody bothered to tell him. Most assume he survived. They were all there. Piggford of the police, Paynter the planter, the Finnellis who were Baptist missionaries – 'she being an artist and a very good tap dancer.'

Such a passage, of course, owes more than a stylistic debt to Scott Fitzgerald. Its stress on 'casual tragedies', its inventory-like evocation of those who participated in the circus-like mood of Nuwara Eliya, the rendition of character through a name ('Piggford of the police, Paynter the planter') or a single defining phrase (' "she being an artist and a very good tap dancer" ') and above all the view of these carefree hedonists as beautiful and damned all suggest the intertextual presence of Fitzgerald. It is a presence which firmly discountenances the view that this past is being seen through rose-coloured glasses.

So 'literary' texts also play a part in the attempt to document 'historical relations'. These can either be works by locals or 'Karapothas'. In the former category there are references to the poet Lakdasa Wikkramasinha and to ancient 'graffiti poems' (p. 84) of the fifth century BC; in the latter the responses to Sri Lanka of Edward Lear, D.H. Lawrence and Leonard Woolf are all quoted (p. 78), and there are also references to numerous other 'foreign' writers who have found literary sustenance in myths about the island. Of these various figures only Leonard Woolf and Robert Knox, who was held prisoner on the island for twenty years and whose book *An Historical Relation* provided a source for *Robinson Crusoe*, are seen as having 'truly [known] where they were' (p. 83). The keynote of European versions of Sri Lanka is exotic mythologization of the kind that Edward Said writes about in *Orientalism*, and this is viewed as inform-ing even European cartographical constructions of the island (pp. 63–4):

> At the edge of the maps the scrolled mantling depicts ferocious slipper-footed elephants, a white queen offering a necklace to natives who carry tusks and a conch, a Moorish king who stands amidst the power of books and armour. On the south-west corner of some charts are satyrs, hoof deep in foam, listening to the sound of the island, their tails writhing in the waves.
>
> The maps reveal rumours of topography, the routes for invasion and trade, and the dark mad mind of travellers' tales appears throughout Arab and Chinese and medieval records. The island seduced all of Europe. The Portuguese. The Dutch. The English. And so its name changed, as well as its shape, – Serendip, Ratnapida ('island of gems'), Taprobane, Zeloan, Zeilan, Seyllan, Ceilon, and Ceylon – the wife of many marriages, courted by invaders who stepped ashore and claimed everything with the power of their sword or bible or language.

Cartographical and linguistic relations are thus seen as just as problematic as historical relations, equally subject to the ideological impositions of culturally partial views. Immediately before this passage the narrator has commented on the changing shape of the island on early maps. Later he gives his own version of the shape it is now accepted as having – 'Ceylon falls on a map and its outline is the shape of a tear' (p. 147) – and in so doing shows his poetic imagination constructing another very partial identity for the island.

Language is, as always, the medium through which all the text's con-structions of place, the past and identity more generally are realized and, in keeping with its postmodernist stance, *Running in the Family* frequently fore-grounds aspects of the signification process. Early on in a passage which describes his response to the East before his return, the narrator records his reaction to the signifier 'Asia' (p. 22):

> *Asia.* The name was a gasp from a dying mouth. An ancient word that had to be whispered, would never be used as a battle cry. The word sprawled. It had none of the clipped sound of Europe, America, Canada. The vowels took over, slept on the mat with the *S*. I was running to Asia and every-thing would change.

Throughout there is the sense that it is language which shapes and can trans-form lives: a vitriolic feud between the narrator's father and a member of another prominent local family has been conducted in the pages of a roadhouse 'visitors' book' (p. 151); the collapse of his mother's handwriting accompanies the breakdown of her marriage, which forces her 'to cope with a new dark unknown alphabet' (p. 150). The interrelatedness of language and cultural identity comes across most forcibly of all in a passage on the Sinhalese alphabet, which is presented as distinctively different from the Sanskrit (p. 83):

> I still believe the most beautiful alphabet was created by the Sinhalese. The insect of ink curves into a shape that is almost sickle, spoon, eyelid. The letters are washed blunt glass which betray no jaggedness. Sanskrit was governed by verticals, but its sharp grid features were not possible in Ceylon. Here the Ola leaves which people wrote on were too brittle. A straight line would cut apart the leaf and so a curling alphabet was derived from its Indian cousin. Moon coconut. The bones of a lover's spine.

As one reads these words and becomes aware of a self-referential element – there is a similarly cursive, poetic quality in the prose, even though the text is confined to English apart from a few illustrations of Sinhalese characters and words at this point – one cannot help but recognize some of the characteristics of *Running in the Family* as essentially Sinhalese. Elsewhere the kind of comic anecdotage with which the work abounds has also been identified as a mode of discourse typical of a certain stratum of Sri Lankan society. Now the qualities that Ondaatje's writing exhibits seem to be fundamentally related to his ancestral origins.

Yet, even while saying this, one has slight reservations for the text takes comparatively little cognizance of the larger society beyond the cloistered world of the socially privileged. This problem is not, however, entirely neglected. In a section entitled 'Don't Talk to Me about Matisse' the issue of the relationship between a privileged culture and the experience of the people becomes the main subject. A poem by Lakdasa Wikkramasinha gives this section its title and is quoted in the text. It dramatizes this relationship in terms of the link between high culture and imperialist brutality (pp. 85–6):

> Don't talk to me about Matisse . . .
> the European style of 1900, the tradition of the studio
> where the nude woman reclines forever
> on a sheet of blood
>
> Talk to me instead of the culture generally –
> how the murderers were sustained
> by the beauty robbed of savages: to our remote
> villages the painters came, and our white-washed
> mud-huts were splattered with gunfire.

*Running in the Family* does move beyond 'the tradition of the studio', beyond art for art's sake in this section, particularly in poems which attempt to portray the experiences of the struggling Sri Lankan masses; but elsewhere the text remains curiously innocent of politics, more interested in presenting the author's grandmother as a 'lyrical socialist' (p. 122) than contemplating 'historical relations' of another kind, those between his privileged family and 'the culture generally'.

Finally its subject is the returned 'prodigal's' relationship to his family and country. Ondaatje stops short of sentimentalizing either, gradually stripping away the comic facade of the family-narrative to reveal a group of people leading lives of not-so-quiet desperation and presenting the country as a poisoned Paradise (p. 81). One wishes that the text had gone further and explored the relationship between the discourse in terms of which the family have constructed their lives and that of the Lakdasa Wikkramasinha poem. But to ask for this is to ask for a different kind of text. *Running in the Family* moves between the twin poles of an essentially apolitical Canadian postmodernist discourse and the conventions of the gently cursive Sinhalese alphabet.

## Notes

1  *The Sons of Captain Poetry*, 1970 film.
2  See my articles 'Beyond History: Margaret Atwood's *Surfacing* and Robert Kroetsch's *Badlands*', in Shirley Chew (ed.), *Re-Visions of Canadian Literature*, edited, Leeds Institute for Bibliographical and Textual Studies, University of Leeds, 1985, pp. 71–87; and 'Acknowledging Myths: The Image of Europe in *The Diviners* and *The Invention of the World*', *Commonwealth*, 10: 1, 1987, pp. 15–21.
3  *Running in the Family*, Toronto, McClelland and Stewart, 1982, p. 39. Subsequent references are to this edition and are cited in the text.
4  *Wide Sargasso Sea*, Harmondsworth, Penguin, 1968, p. 63.
5  Aldous Huxley, *Collected Essays*, New York, Harper & Row, 1959, pp. 1–10.
6  For a Canadian commentary on paternalistic models of influence see Shirley Neuman and Robert Wilson, *Labyrinths of Voice: Conversations with Robert Kroetsch*, Edmonton, NeWest Press, 1982, pp. 20ff.
7  See particularly Roland Barthes, *The Pleasure of the Text*, trans. Richard Miller, New York, Hill and Wang, 1975.
8  See particularly the accounts of Gatsby's parties and the guests who attend them at the beginning of Chapters 3 and 4 of F. Scott Fitzgerald *The Great Gatsby*, New York, Charles Scribner's Sons, 1925.

# 5

# Burning Down the House:
# Neil Bissoondath's Fiction

## David Richards

The term 'Commonwealth literature' has become increasingly unfashionable as its panopticon disciplinary force has been dispersed by appropriately indecisive alternatives: new literatures or postcolonial writings. The shift is not simply a matter of the periodic and theory-led transformations the subject has been heir to: there is also an acknowledgement that the maps of the world have radically altered. Commonwealth literature was a fundamentally dialogical form of interpretation where 'other voices' held a dialogue – linguistic, metaphoric, fictional, cultural – with a centrally located tradition of literary and critical materials. That the debate was hardly ever equal has led to its replacement by alternatives which do not stress the perceived peripheral nature of non-metropolitan writings. Yet it is also the case that increasingly the notion of dialogue does not fit the new conditions of authorship. The Empire, however transformed, no longer conducts a dialogue with its erstwhile masters: the dualistic notion of the Commonwealth as constituting a centre and periphery has been displaced by writers who are situated in a triangulation of different locations: V.S. Naipaul draws his topographical projections from India to Trinidad to England: Jamaica Kincaide from Africa, the Caribbean to America: Michael Ondaatje from Sri Lanka to England to Canada. The triangular-shaped world requires a redrawing of the old maps, a new orientation to historical time and a retelling of the myths of origin.

This essay is principally concerned with Neil Bissoondath's fictions, which deal with transformations in space, time and narrative and the unique role of Canada in shaping such a triangular world. Superimposed on the three locations he evokes – India, Casaquemada (a fictional Caribbean Island) and

Canada – are triangles of space, time and narrative. This is not simply the naive realism of which Bissoondath has been accused, of reflecting uncritically upon the relationship of narrative to time and space. Behind that triangular relationship lies a highly problematic discussion of the nature of representation, of tradition and of postcolonial identity.

Alone in his study, Raj, the narrator of *A Casual Brutality*, contemplates the maps of India, Casaquemada and Canada which cover the walls of the room. The maps crystallize many of the latent themes of the novel. As pictures, as decoration, they prefigure the photographs of Toronto's Kensington Market which another Casaquemadan, the ill fated Kayso, pins up in his room. Like those photographs they are also forms of representation which the novel will increasingly challenge. In addition, the form of the map is a representation of codes of meaning which possess elocutionary force, special signs which will be found to be increasingly unfathomable. As emblems of space and time the maps tell stories, narratives which correspond to Raj's and Bissoondath's past, present and future. But the maps are an index, not of the situation of the self located in time and space, defining and defined by the otherness which coheres around it, but of an opposite tendency. The map is a symbol of splitting and division and the consequences of history (p. 312):

> My eyes travelled east across Africa, through the middle East, past the Arabian Sea to the cone of the Indian Subcontinent. Then, searching, the way back by sea: south through the Indian Ocean past Madagascar, around the cape of Good Hope into the South Atlantic: north – cutting a path between South America and the west coast of Africa – up to the Caribbean, past Trinidad up the chain to the wobbly red circle that marked Casaquemada.

The many locations of the maps are rendered into a few key sites as Raj's visual journey mimics the historical voyages of his ancestors, the indentured labourers of the subcontinent. Raj continues but does not complete the migration of his ancestors to the North Atlantic and Canada. Since the first act of *King Lear*, the map has been the image of domination, the world rendered as representation, for consumption or destruction. But Raj holds no such dominion: space is ungraspable and contradictory: too large, too small (p. 34):

> I am, by birth, Casaquemadan: by necessity disguised as choice, Canadian. There was Canada, there was Casaquemada, the one unseizably massive, the other unseizably minute.

Spatial representations evoke a crisis of identity in the relocated narrator who cannot bring the maps to signify his situation. Just as in a short story Bissoondath writes that 'a person moved, was driven by a spasm beyond human control like a piece of meat moving through intestine',[1] and 'It is a version, more tragic, of continental drift'.[2] Bissoondath's own narrative identity is similarly modelled on the contingent fictional identities he evokes. Raj's dislocation begs the question of authorial situation: into what context can these texts be inserted? In which of the maps' topographies would these writings constitute a significant landmark? India, the Caribbean, Canada?

As it is with space, so it is with time as the history of the dislocated will not take significant shape. Bissoondath's list of characters is a rollcall of those dispossessed of their history: their origins conspire to frame their destruction or compel their flight.

> I lost myself on the roads, rivers and names of the maps the way one can lose oneself – the past, the present, the future, one's very being – in the slow, steady mesmerizing movements of fish in an aquarium.[3]

The stories repeat the failed attempts of characters to fix the 'fluid holding pattern' of time and to make coherent historical narratives of maps which do not dissolve into absurdity, negation and violence. Bissoondath's characters live with a past which has 'formed but does not inform'.[4] Even the inherited images of India acquire the contours of a dark myth which is distant and unavailable. In 'Digging Up the Mountains', Hari Beharry holds Biswasian hopes for his new home as the site where time and place may chime:

> It was in this house that Hari planned to entertain his grandchildren and their children, to this house that he would welcome future Beharry hordes, from this house that he would be buried. This house spoke of generations.[5]

The continuity of the Indian patriarchy in the New World, a version of the past stretching into and structuring the future, life on a minor epic scale, 'now', as Bissoondath comments, 'seemed absurd'.[6]

'Time', Bissoondath writes, almost as an admission that the postcolonial cannot know history, only 'time'.

> Time kaleidoscopes. The past is refracted back and forth becomes the present, is highlightened by it, is illuminated by it, is replaced by it. In this rush of sparkle and eclipse, only the future is obscured, predictability shattered. Yesterday becomes today, today steps back from itself, and tomorrow might never be.[7]

When time is substituted for history, Bissoondath's characters are subject to the unpredictability of the endless present tense when even 'today steps back from itself'.

Time and space are, of course, the coordinates most adhered to by realist narratives and myths of origin. The world is given its density by the sense that we begin in such a place and at such a time, lending a tangible authority to acts of naming. The fictional Caribbean island of *A Casual Brutality* is located by a myth of origins and naming in an immediately post-Columbus era (p. 37):

> The Spanish captain, a man not totally devoid of compassion, ordered that a hut be constructed of tree branches for the malcontent, a man of

disputatious character named Lopez. Three months later, the captain once more put in at the island to see whether the malcontent had learned his lesson. He found that Lopez had set fire to the hut around himself, his blackened skeleton propped up, as if lounging in comfort, against a scorched beam in the centre of the ashen ruins. In his log, the captain had penned a brief entry: 'Casa quemada'. House burnt. 'Lopez muerto'. Lopez dead. And so, from these simple words, brutal in their brevity yet inconsequential among the thousands he had scribbled in his impatient script, the island got its name and its embryonic myth.

Lopez, expelled from human society, initiates history as suicide in a reiteration of the Hobbesian paradigm: 'simple', 'brutal', 'brief', 'inconsequential'. For the Spanish captain the tale seems hardly worth the telling. The island's myth of origins evokes the Edenic genesis while at the same time enacting a perverse denial of its elocutionary authority. In the short story, 'There are Lots of Ways to Die', a failed historian of Casaquemada recounts his reason for failure: it is not because of a failure of ability but 'because our history doesn't lead anywhere. It's just a big black hole. Nobody's interested in a book about a hole.'[8]

Incapable of history and the justifying charters of myth the island is doomed to repeat *ad infinitum* the conditions of its origins. Any modern Lopez, noisy and intractable, is a problem to be solved by a method imported from South American dictatorships, but perfectly recalling the island's myth of origins. Trouble makers are taken to the remote forests and a small house of logs and twigs, big enough to hold a man, is built next to a tree. A chain is attached at one end to the tree, at the other end it is secured around the man's genitals. A razor is provided. The house is set on fire. The options are simple, brutal, brief and inconsequential – cut or burn.[9]

To date Bissoondath's writings have been explorations of these themes: incoherent space, the disintegration of an already fractured past, voices speaking in a void, a drift towards an incipient violence, the flight to security in Canada and the life of an emasculated immigrant. All his narratives deal, in varying shades, with people caught between cutting or burning: Bissoondath's narrative world is charted between those two polar regions. Redemption comes in the shape of those who return to Casaquemada from exile in Toronto; they have messianic fervour but compromised ministries. Kayso, the civil rights lawyer who campaigned against police brutality, meets his calvary electrocuted by a 'life-size electric sex-doll'.[10]

Yet this is not to suggest that the triangulation of space, time and myth do not produce narratives which make a sense of the past cohere into a realized historical vision. At the climax of the novel *A Casual Brutality*, Casaquemada jerks into an even more extensive spasm of random violence and police massacres. While Raj attends to his dying grandfather, the police raid his home and kill his Canadian wife and three-year-old son. Raj, in a state of anguished bewilderment, finds himself at the old colonial fort in the hills above Lopez City (pp. 366–7):

And I felt that somehow those men who had sweated and strained here, making their little play at fortification only, just over a century and a half later, to cut their losses and run in a well-orchestrated theatre of brass-bands and flag-raising, were in no small measure responsible for the fact that my wife and my son were dead, that my home was a shambles, that Madera [a policeman], gun in hand, was down there somehow satisfying his bloodlust. Those men who had sweated and strained had had other, more valuable lessons to teach, but they had paid only lip-service to their voiced ideals, had offered in the end but the evils of their actions, had propagated but the baser instincts, which took root and flourished so effortlessly in this world they called, with a kind of black humour, *new*.

If these two sentences are meant to account for the lacuna in the history of the dislocated, and if this is Raj's portion of truth – that Casaquemada is a failed experiment in nationhood, one of many, grasping at all the vices of colonial pedagogy, ignoring all its virtues, the place the colonialists 'overlooked' (in both senses of the word) – then it is, however true, ultimately painfully banal. Its elocutionary force derives from a naive, even simplistic realism: a strict linearity of historical mechanics connecting chains of events from cause to ultimate effects: from Lopez to murdered wife and child. As if the apocalypse of Casaquemada was present in and sprung from its genesis. If this fundamentalism contained all of Bissoondath's message then adverse criticism of his work would have found its justification. But it does not: behind the triangulation of space, time and myth lie the further, more problematic dimensions of representation, tradition and identity, which counter and overwhelm the texts' fundamentalist realism.

Raj's myth of the fall of Casaquemada is only the threshold from which it is possible to begin to elaborate a counterpoint to imperialism's dominant ideological categories. To the dislocated, representation is a lie: art, Bissoondath seems to feel, has the potential to be the most pernicious of lies since it is willed self-delusion.

Victoria Jackson, the expatriate teacher of 'An Arrangement of Shadows', contemplates the landscape of the Caribbean island shortly before she commits suicide, islands and suicide forming a terrible objective correlative in Bissoondath's work as the 'not being' of suicide comes to correspond to the 'no place' or 'black hole' of the island:

> The landscape – how foreign a word it now seemed, since she had come to think of it with the local phrase as simply 'The Hills' – this landscape, once viewed as a possible watercolour, failed to revive her, depressed her a little more even.
>
> She had lost her sense of the picturesque. Despite herself, she had learnt quickly that the picturesque existed not by itself but in a quiet self-delusion, in that warping of observation which convinced the mind that in poverty was beauty, in atrophy quaintness, the hovel a hut.[11]

Victoria's disclosure of the failure of representation is close to what John

Moss had identified as a 'discovery' made by Canadian poets that 'their inability to establish a lyric presence within the Canadian landscape had more to do with the nature of language than with the natural world or with the authenticity of their experience within it'.[12] For the dislocated, mimetic forms – the 'hills' and their associated representations of landscape, watercolour, the picturesque – are not merely inauthentic representations, misrecognitions, but 'writings' in a different script, alien languages forgotten or unlearned. This self is not discovered in, nor recognized by, art. It is only in the radical subversion of art, art subjected to violence, clinically violated or riotously delimbed, that the misrecognized image can be turned to gesture at the site of enunciation: 'Through the door ahead of her the hills, their ugliness bared that morning by brilliance like disease by a scalpel'[13].

Bissoondath's islanders and Toronto immigrants are constantly reminded that they are bounded by mimesis, inhabiting representations or metaphors of the self as the reflected vehicles of constructed models. The fiction of time and place, of myths of origin, is a form of mimicry, for 'to accept this life was to accept second place. A man who had tasted first could accept second only with delusion.'[14] The 'second place' of island life acquires the status of art as something made, a fiction or a 'delusion' of misrepresentation. Joseph the businessman returned to his island in the story 'Insecurity' only to discover that 'You couldn't claim the island: it claimed you', enlisting him in its fiction like – just like – a character in a short story:

> The island of his birth, on which he had grown up and where he had made his fortune, was transformed by a process of mind into a kind of temporary home. Its history ceased to be important: its present turned into a fluid holding pattern which would eventually give way.[15]

Hari Beharry muses on attempting to fix the 'fluid holding pattern' into the forms of fiction in acts of naming: 'He started thinking about giving [this house] a name, like a ranch: Middlemarch, Rancho Rico, Golden Bough.'[16] Bissoondath's irony subverts these mimetic rites, gently as in Hari's case, more acerbically in the case of the acronyms invented by Trinidadian revolutionaries: 'You ever hear about the Popular Insurrection Service Squad? Or the Caribbean Region Association of Patriots?'[17] The comic subversions of fantasies of belonging and grotesque political action transform the 'local colour' of the exotic mimic into absurdity and negation. What trajectory, other than absurdity and negation, is described by Raj's grandfather's story of the island dance contest won by a one-legged man with a crutch? His prize was a brand new bicycle. Or his Uncle Grappler's more sombre version of Casaquemadan history as the achievement of independence and, hence, 'the right to do nothing'? Increasingly, the fictions turn to the madman Sunil, whose vision of the human race is one of people 'talking about freedom and light but . . . in its fear, in a queer perversion of its vision, welcomed slavery and darkness'.[18]

The question of tradition becomes a fraught matter for Bissoondath, in the sense that any dialogue with an English literary tradition would reduplicate the tropes of misrepresentation if there were not also an attendant subversion of that tradition. A contradictory triangulation is established between the tradition, its evocation and its denial. I asked earlier, into what context can these texts be inserted? In which of the maps would they constitute a significant landmark? The answer is all and none, for the writing evokes a dominant tradition with its attendant forms of realism and linearity, only to expose its capacity for misrepresentation, failure and delusion. Bissoondath is hardly alone in this: it is a feature which has also marked the work of his uncle, V.S. Naipaul. Both writers share an appetite for a terrible comedy, an ironizing of futility. Naipaul's legacy is also found in Bissoondath's adoption of images of the human body as an index of a wider human malaise. The masticating mouths dribbling food and the frank revelations of a Toronto stripper seem congruent with a Swiftian impulse which both writers share. But above all, if Naipaul's Jimmy Ahmed, in *Guerrillas* (1975) could be said to have decisively terminated the tenuous and ambiguous accommodation of Mr Biswas, then Bissoondath takes up the story of unaccommodated man's failing struggle against the arsonist. *A Casual Brutality*, recalling the island's genesis myth, depicts the burning of *A House for Mr Biswas*.

A more extravagant notion of literary tradition can be gathered from the Caribbean writer, critic, historian, cricket connoisseur and Marxist theorist C.L.R. James, in his characteristically provocative relocations of authorial identity:

> The first West Indian writer whom I know of is one of the most famous novelists who ever lived: Alexandre Dumas. He never went to the West Indies, but in everything that really matters he is a West Indian writer.[19]

James's claim on Dumas partly relies upon Dumas's grandfather owning a plantation and keeping a black mistress in Haiti. But, 'what really matters' and what makes Dumas West Indian for James, is his bringing of history within the scope of narrative. A belief that history can be comprehended, mapped, by the cartography of nineteenth-century Romance. In a sense what Dumas shares with the West Indies, Bissoondath shares with Canada, since the changed coordinates of the historical map transform narrative representation from historical romance, which compels events to cohere into significance, to the postmodern fiction which has become the modern world's experience of its history. The kind of dislocated, dispossessed and misrepresented vision which Bissoondath evokes is a view of a landscape which Canadian writers have claimed as their own territory. 'Canada is a postmodern country . . . our genealogy is postmodern'[20].

The riddles of history continue to possess their teasing and irritant force causing an 'incredulity toward metanarratives'[21]. 'Canada' is a condition, a postmodern condition of the radically dispossessed inheritors of modernism's fragmented vision for whom the world's maps and messages will not cohere into versions of Romance. All of Bissoondath's writings lay claim to that most Canadian of narrative material. Together with Atwood and Kroetsch, Bissoondath explores the unavailability of an adequate narrative of origins while, simultaneously, utilizing those systems of narration which place priority on the evocation of precisely those myths of origin. As with Atwood and Kroetsch, Bissoondath interrogates the forms of representation and narrative which make for such priorities: mythical discourses are scrutinized, parodied, dissolved, rendered objects of play or *rites de passage*. Yet unlike Atwood and Kroetsch, the questioning of the frame of narrative means for Bissoondath the 'crossing' of postmodernism's narratives with postcolonial representations. This is not the 'play of discourses'; as Homi Bhabha wrote in a different context, Bissoondath conjures 'the evil eye that seeks to outstare linear history and turn its progressive dream into nightmarish chaos'[22]. The dislocated postcolonial subject (Indian–West Indian–Canadian) inhabits a postmodern fiction of unmeasurable distances ('unseizably large/unseizably minute'), anti-Cartesian scepticism ('I lost myself'), in a 'Canada' which defies situation and thereby transforms postmodernist play into postcolonial pain.

Bissoondath's strength comes from his illuminations of a postcolonial subjectivity which is admitted only restricted areas of representation within the binary codes of colonialism's manichean mimesis: white, black: possessor, dispossessed. In Toronto Raj sees abundant examples of the ways in which the dislocated subject contrives to manipulate his own representation (p. 221):

> I had not come to toronto to find Casaquemada, or to play the role of ethnic, deracinated and costumed, drawing around him the defensive postures of the land left behind. And this display of the rakish, this attempt at third world exoticism, seemed to me a trap, a way of sealing the personality, of rendering it harmless to all but the individual.

The I which speaks here is both intriguing and instructive since it speaks by what it disavows. Its elocutionary force derives from a denial of a voice. The alternative to the mimicry of 'playing the role of the ethnic', substituting self with representation, cannot be said to exist except as a negation of that representation. The dislocated subject carries with him to Toronto the Casaquemadan solution – cut or burn – trim the self into a shaped misrepresentation ('deracinated and costumed') or seek consuming negation. But just as Raj refuses 'to play the role of ethnic', and wear an off the peg representation so Bissoondath is faced with the same dilemma. How can narrative escape representation without fleeing towards negation? Is Bissoondath's work an exercise in negation which comprehends its own inability to unveil the totality of character or which presents us, alternatively, with a manipulated representation? Does Bissoondath cut or burn? Or is it possible for fiction to emanate from a place which is always 'not'? A voice which makes, but is not 'in' its narrative? His narrative will not cohere into a unity which lends identity to its subjects. His language constantly reaches for the negative form. Not what is, but what is not: denial, negation, the mirror's reflection. In so doing, Bissoondath lays bare what Homi Bhabha (following Fanon) has described as the 'perverse palimpsest of colonial identity'[23], which uses words, as Raj says, not as tools of enquiry, but in their most dangerous capacity, as agents of concealment. Bissoondath's writing perpetually attempts to uncover the true nature of the postcolonial while at the same time acknowledging that writing protects and hides, effaces the colonized self.

Writing such as Bissoondath's assumes a large degree of detachment. This is not the same as Arnoldian 'disinterestedness' but a more problematic strategy of obliqueness both to the subject and form of the fiction. Fiction which attempts to lend a voice to those who are voiceless in accents which are necessarily someone else's ('picturesque' or 'rakish') must be circumspect. In 'Digging Up The Mountains', Bissoondath writes of this sense of necessity, in producing fictions which are always incomplete, unresolved: 'All in passing . . . visions fraught with the insubstantial, footnotes forming of themselves no whole, offering but image and sensation as recompense for endless motion.'[24]

One such offering of image and sensation is delivered in the story 'There Are Lots of Ways to Die', where the friend of a friend is found dead 'in the washroom of a Cinema. A girl was with him. Naked. She wasn't dead. She's in a madhouse now.'[25] Another footnote to an unrecoverable story.

The place they occupy becomes an 'ellipsis'[26], a syntactical figure of omission, between two statements: an implied but unrealized presence. Recalling the failed historian, Bissoondath writes 'books about a hole': a black hole from which a voice emanates. He elevates the syntactical figure to a rhetorical figure for, by evoking lives disrupted by the random events of 'kaleidoscopic time', the unpredictable and disruptive are the very means by which his writing reveals, not the subject himself, but the acts of concealment effacing that identity. This subject can only be evoked by the negative values of language: Bissoondath's characters exist in the interstices, the 'gaps' between narratives of origin, places of residence, representations of the self. Bissoondath thus cuts through the banality of Raj's historical construction to offer a vision of colonial identity which is anything but banal.

Frantz Fanon, Hannah Arendt, Jan Mohamed and Homi Bhabha have variously identified colonialism's destructive mission as a substitution of an image of dominance and imperial power for the colonized sense of otherness; an intervention in and distortion of the enabling process of identity by substituting a narrowing and delimiting image of imperial power for the enabling evolution of civil societies, legal systems, languages, cultures. Bissoondath presents a much more complex formulation. His vision of the postcolonial condition is not that of a simple distortion of self and other which requires the removal of imperialism's distorting mirror to return the colonial subject to his rightful manicheism. For Bissoondath colonial intervention, migration, dislocation and neglect have wrought a perpetuating sense of fracture which continues to fragment both self and other. In Fanon's phrase, 'a constellation of delirium' enacts and re-enacts a tragic cycle from which no recuperation is possible and which renders the colonial subject silent, invisible and unformed, since language, law, civil society, culture consist of the replicated divisions of colonial identity. Bissoondath's dispossessed live in an 'alienated image of man', where the 'otherness of the self' makes the Casaquemadan solution – cut or burn – the only one which obtains. As Homi Bhabha writes, if 'the [colonial] subject of desire is never simply a Myself, then the Other is never simply an It-self, a font of identity, truth or mis-recognition.'[27] What is returned to us is fragmentation, delirium, isolation: the postmodern world where play is turned to pain.

Vernon, the central character of the story 'Veins Visible', has a dream which conjures the terrible but appropriate image of the *corps morcelé*,[28] the self envisioned as a mutilated, truncated torso:

> Then as if it was the most natural thing in the world, he found himself lying on the sidewalk looking up at the sky, ink blue with curls of diaphonous white cloud. That something was not right he was fully aware, but only when he tried to get up did he realise that his torso had been severed diagonally from just under his ribcage to the small of his back. His hips and legs lay two feet away, beyond reach, like the discarded lower half of a mannequin. Curious, he examined his lower half. The cut had been clean. There was no blood. The wound appeared to have been coated in clear plastic and he would see the ends of veins pulsing red against the transparent skin. There was, he knew, no danger.[29]

The *corps morcelé* recurs throughout Bissoondath's writings as people are framed in windows, caught in photographs, rendered in portraits, searched for in maps, but in part, 'footnotes forming of themselves no whole'.[30] (This is, in a sense, to make these grim images more sombre, since there is a joke of kinds in the long quotation above: 'his hips and legs lay *two feet* away . . .') Likewise, the texts themselves are *morcelé*, disjunctive, abridged, mutilated in imitation of the situation of the dislocated. Their repeated journeyings between Casaquemada and Toronto, the framings of image and action show a totality which is cut, redistributed and unavailable to the novel and stories. The narrative presents framed images which open on to other frames of truncated information receding into opacity.[31] These framed, truncated images disrupt the strident linear narrative with a different counter-rhythm causing it to stumble over obstacles laid in its path. 'It was Hari. Then it was Peter. Then Hari again. Then it was no one again. Just a man. The man had no arms. Despair.'[32]

The unelaborated sense of self is disclosed by omission as the dispossessed views himself as an object discoursing on its strangeness: 'I notice that I notice', or on the blankness of its social constructions: 'I do not lead. I never have. I have practised only avoidance.' The world of the postcolonial subject is a subjunctive state, viewed obliquely, tilted at an angle: 'Everything seems to have rounded corners, everything seems somehow soft'. 'Life swimming in delusion, life shimmering in fantasy'.[33] The constant replication of division which marks the postcolonial identity is most powerfully conveyed by the refugee who waits for his wife at the airport, twenty years after the unnamed war which pulled them apart:

> It was like viewing, in rapid succession, the positive and negative of the

same photograph: the vision was tricked, the substantial lost, so that even the angular concrete of the airport car park across the way was emptied, became unreal.[34]

It is difficult, therefore, to know how to conclude: to summarize would be to restore the body to its wholeness, to suture the wound which Bissoondath insists on fingering to inflammation: to render the postcolonial subjunctive an imperial indicative, when the vision, refracted and concave, is contingent, *morcelé*, hypothetical. Better to end in contingent compromise? Raj, in *A Casual Brutality*, begins by stating that 'Self, in the end, is the prime motivation', but, 'in the end', he glimpses his own constellation of delirium. 'So this', he says, 'is how the world shatters, with a peep at the soul.'[35]

Fictional acts of displacement become for Bissoondath the appropriate – the decorous – medium for the expression of a postcolonial vision. At this point I am compelled to go back to James's claiming of Dumas as a West Indian writer. For James the act of claiming had more to do with politics than literary history in that the congruence of history and romance fitted James's sense of political decorum. What political or historical vision descends from Bissoondath's elliptical voices? From his hybrid of Caribbean postcolonialism and Canadian postmodernism?

Bissoondath's voices are always alone, inspected, threatened, lost: the thin ellipsis of the self. Thus isolated from his social role, his class and his community, the individual can neither control the representations language throws up nor embrace its history. The 'fact' of the unavailability of communal languages and historical narratives in the Caribbean and Canada is the process by which the postcolonial subject is 'known' or 'recognized'. Bissoondath's postcolonials cannot break out of the confining parentheses of the ellipsis, nor can they be simply dismissed as 'third world exotics' 'deracinated and costumed'. Yet, paradoxically, this evocation of a state of historylessness is accomplished by calling forth a great deal of history: the house must be constructed for it to be burned. The view of Bissoondath as a naive or simple realist perpetuates the dualistic interpretation of the marginal engaged in dialogue with the centre. It fails to see the third figure, the hungry ghost at the feast, known by what it lacks.

### Notes

1  Neil Bissoondath, 'Man as Plaything, Life as Mockery', in *Digging Up The Mountains* (*DM*), Harmondsworth, Penguin, 1987, p. 178.
2  'Continental Drift', in *DM*, p. 145.
3  Neil Bissoondath, *A Casual Brutality* (*CB*), London, Bloomsbury, 1988, pp. 34–5.
4  *CB*, p. 377.
5  'Digging Up The Mountains', *DM*, p. 14.
6  'Digging Up The Mountains', *DM*, p. 15.
7  *CB*, p. 18.

8  'There are Lots of Ways to Die', *DM*, p. 92.
9  *CB*, p. 211.
10  *CB*, p. 343.
11  'An Arrangement of Shadows', *DM*, p. 112.
12  John Moss, *Invisible in the House of Mirrors*, Canada House Lecture Series Number 21, London, 1983, p. 5.
13  'An Arrangement of Shadows', *DM*, p. 116.
14  'There are Lots of Ways to Die', *DM*, p. 81.
15  'Insecurity', *DM*, p. 72.
16  'Digging Up The Mountains', *DM*, p. 5.
17  'The Revolutionary', *DM*, p. 26.
18  *CB*, p. 178.
19  Ian Munro and Reinhard Sander, (eds), *Kas-Kas, Interviews with Three Caribbean Writers*, African and Afro-American Research Institute, Austin, University of Texas, 1972, p. 23.
20  Robert Kroetsch, 'Disunity as Unity: A Canadian Strategy', in Colin Nicholson and Peter Easingwood (eds), *Canadian History and Story*, Edinburgh, University of Edinburgh Press, 1986, p. 2.
21  Jean-Francois Lyotard, *The Postmodern Condition*, Manchester, Manchester University Press, 1984.
22  Homi K. Bhabha, 'Interrogating Identity', *Identity*, London, ICA Documents 6, 1987, p. 8.
23  Homi K. Bhabha, 'Difference, Discrimination and the Discourse of Colonialism', in F. Barker (ed.), *The Politics of Theory*, Colchester, University of Essex, 1983, p. 121.
24  'Continental Drift', *DM*, p. 148.
25  'There are Lots of Ways to Die', *DM*, p. 90.
26  Homi K. Bhabha, 'Interrogating Identity', p. 9.
27  Homi K. Bhabha, 'Foreword' to Frantz Fanon, *Black Skin, White Masks*, London, Pluto Press, 1980, p. xviii.
28  cf. Jacques Lacan, 'Le Stade du Miroir', in *Ecrits*, Paris, Éditions du Seuil, 1966 and Christine Brooke-Rose, *A Rhetoric of the Unreal*, Cambridge, Cambridge University Press, 1981.
29  'Veins Visible', *DM*, p. 221.
30  'Continental Drift', *DM*, p. 145.
31  cf. Christine Brooke-Rose, 1981, pp. 161–87.
32  'Veins Visible', *DM*, p. 222.
33  'In the Kingdom of the Golden Dust', *DM*, p. 98; 'The Cage', *DM*, p. 67 & p. 57; *CB*, p. 372.
34  'Man as Plaything, Life as Mockery', *DM*, p. 178.
35  *CB*, p. 367.

# 6

# One Cast of a Net: A Reading of
# Daphne Marlatt's *Steveston*

## Shirley Chew

> Yes. This is the only place that I feel I really belong; this is the only city
> on the continent that feels like home. When I came here at the age of
> nine & started walking in the woods for the first time, wore jeans for
> the first time, I realized that this was my place. I made an immediate
> identification with it . . .
>
> Daphne Marlatt, interviewed by George Bowering, in 'Given
> This Body', *Open Letter*, 4th series, 3, Spring 1979, p. 32.

As Marlatt goes on to enlarge upon her attachment to Vancouver, it becomes
clear that between the first spurt of discovery ('immediate identification') and
the settled conviction ('I feel I really belong'), there was a lengthy period of
adaptation and self-searching. This was 'because the immigrant thing was very
strong in me for years and years', so much so that until the early 1970s and,
presumably, the writing of *Vancouver Poems* (1972), it thwarted any deep sense
of community with other west coast writers: 'I never felt that I was part of even
the *Tish* group'.[1] Taking possession of her own life as a person and a poet meant,
among other considerations, coming to terms with and learning to write out of
'the immigrant thing' – that consciousness of being 'perilously on the edge',
neither belonging quite nor extricated entirely, 'in here' yet drawn by all that
lies 'out there'.

Marlatt's position as immigrant has special interest in that, unlike Michael
Ondaatje, for example, she cannot lay claim to an original point of departure.
She was born in Australia where her British parents had been evacuated from
Malaya when a Japanese invasion appeared imminent. The war over, the family
returned to Penang for six years before finally departing, after a brief sojourn in
England, for Vancouver. In their new home, competing loyalties became evident:

> They both [the parents] referred to England as home when I was a child,
> and yet they chose not to go home when they left Penang. I grew up with

two nostalgias in our house: the nostalgia for England, which, having spent only some months there, I didn't really understand; the nostalgia for Penang, which I could share though it was effaced by an enthusiasm for *this* place here.[2]

When Marlatt was born the war in the Pacific had already entered its critical phase. Between December 1941 and April 1942 the Japanese landed in Malaya, bombarded Pearl Harbour, captured Singapore (the 'impregnable fortress', so-called, of the British empire), and then Hong Kong, the Philippines, Burma, the Dutch East Indies and most of the islands of the central and south-west Pacific. The drive behind Japan's military intervention was economic, the creation of the Greater East Asia Co-prosperity Sphere. At the same time many Japanese believed that Japan's mission was to free Asia from Western colonialism and this could only be achieved if it were to become the stabilizing force in the region. Contradictions of this kind, as W.G. Beasley has pointed out, are 'inherent in the nature of empire' and are, in this instance, the less surprising when we bear in mind that Japanese imperialism developed partly out of a sense of national danger in the face of Western attempts to curb its economic enterprise, especially within China and South-east Asia.[3] What I wish to suggest is that, given Marlatt's immigrant consciousness, the dark vision of her long poem, *Steveston*, arises from her apprehension of the deadly struggle in the Pacific which coincided with the early years of her existence, as well as her insights into the history of the Japanese fishermen and their families who lived through the anti-Asiatic feelings and activities of white Canadians in the first half of the century.

In 1972 Marlatt became involved in an aural history project at the University of British Columbia which sought to understand the role of the Japanese–Canadians in Steveston. As a method for studying the recent past, aural history claims to extend 'the limits of historical documentation' by making available 'the thoughts, feelings, and life-stories of the individuals who are the very substance of that history'.[4] The book which came out of the project, *Steveston Recollected: A Japanese–Canadian History* (1975), edited by Daphne Marlatt, aimed therefore at retaining the immediacy and flexibility of the original method by juxtaposing different kinds of evidence – transcriptions and translations of taped interviews, commentaries by the editor, photographs both archival and up to date, written records, statistics. The image it puts across of the place as seen from the point of view of its Japanese community is a solid one: the faltering, mean beginnings; the gradually improved quality of life that had its concrete signs in the boats owned, houses built, the Japanese Fishermen's Hospital, the Fishermen's Co-op, the Fishermen's Association; then, following Pearl Harbor in December 1941, the swift reversal in the form of evacuation and internment as 'enemies of the state'; finally the slow drift back from 1949 onwards and the new prosperity.

As it turns out, *Steveston Recollected* is less revealing than might be expected.

While the *issei* and *nisei* (first and second generation Japanese–Canadians) were fully prepared to recount the practical concerns and circumstances of their lives as fishermen, cannery workers, 'enemy aliens', they were generally unwilling, whether from policy or habit, to voice their reactions to hostile treatment and hardship. The emphasis is upon survival, rehabilitation and the material achievements of recent years, and the thrust of the narrative is positive and optimistic. This impression is reinforced by the chronological progression of the work which takes the reader from 1899, the year the oldest of the *issei* interviewed arrived in Steveston, to 1973, the date appended to the last of Marlatt's commentaries; and by the cyclical pattern of the narrated history. The sectional headings suitably read: 'From boat boss to house boss', 'Fishing in the old days'/ 'Fishing today', 'Early Steveston'/'Evacuation and internment camp'/'Return to Steveston'. 'Were you bitter, angry?' But such feelings, if they did occur and if they still prevail, are glossed over with a smile, a joke, gestures of acceptance ('It was the war'), of evasion ('Old people don't like to talk about the past'). It is this silence which Marlatt sets out to interpret and fill so that, without ceasing to be Japanese–Canadian history, *Steveston* (1974), the long poem, becomes also her story.[5]

Investigating the characteristics of the genre, Dorothy Livesay dubbed the Canadian long poem 'the documentary poem', on account of the conscious attempt it makes 'to create a dialectic between the objective facts and the subjective feelings of the poet'.[6] The ineptness of the term 'documentary' has been probed by Frank Davey in a recent discussion of different approaches 'to achieving "truth" in poetry':

> I doubt that there are any purely 'documentary' poems. Regardless of the
> poet's intentions or aesthetics, the documents he appropriates . . . serve
> at best as a ground against which his own work grows, as a countertext, a
> substructure, a provocation to his own words, and entry for them into
> history.[7]

By looking in some detail at *Steveston*, the long poem, and with passing references to *Steveston Recollected*, the documented evidence, I hope to draw attention to the narrative strategies which enabled, in Marlatt's case, that 'provocation to her own words'.

> Imagine: a town
> Imagine a town running
> (smoothly?)
> a town running before a fire
> canneries burning
> (do you see the shadow of charred stilts
> on cool water? do you see enigmatic chance standing
> just under the beam?
> He said they were playing cards in the

Chinese mess hall, he said it was dark (a hall? a shack.
they were all, crowded together on top of each other.
He said somebody accidentally knocked the oil lamp over, off
the edge
                        where stilts are standing, Over the edge of the
dyke a river pours, uncalled for, unending:
                                        where chance lurks
fishlike, shadows the underside of pilings, calling up his hall
the bodies of men & fish corpse piled on top of each other (residue
time is, the delta) rot, an endless waste the trucks of production
grind to juice, driving through
                        smears, blood smears in the dark
dirt) this marshland silt no graveyard can exist in but water swills
endlessly out of itself to the mouth
                                ringed with residue, where
chance flicks his tail & swims, through

As the poem opens, the imagination, grappling with town and with language,
matter and medium, uncovers a pair of stories – of success, of disaster.
Jettisoning the one for the time being, the narrative plunges into the midst of
'canneries burning'. Gone are the decorous structures of *Steveston Recollected*
and instead the precarious nature of this Steveston evinces itself in the poem's
discontinuities of form and the mixedness of its textual fabric. First, there is the
constant overlap of verse and prose with unusual strands of sound cutting
across familiar patterns of words – cards, crowded, mess hall, were all, dark,
shack, together, each other. Second, there is the restless play of genres – myth,
epic, history; of styles – the performative verve of oral narrative, the calculated
steps of reportage, the concentration of lyric; of voices – seer, raconteur,
elegist. Third, there are the dislocations of syntax that lay open the multiple,
often conflicting, possibilities of language – just as 'a town running before a
fire' combines the ideas of efficient functioning previous to disaster and flight
from disaster, so scarcely impeded by endstop marks, 'fire' runs into 'river'
(mingling, for a brief moment, flames and water), and 'unending' river into
'endless waste' (of flooding and of industry). Caught from its earliest days
between human folly and natural calamities, Steveston is a gamble. Viewed
from the 'underside of pilings' rather than the frontage of history books, its
presiding deity is not human will and effort but chance in its many guises –
'enigmatic' as a buddha, inimical as Pluto and elusive as the salmon upon which
the fortunes of the town rest.

One of the sections in *Steveston Recollected*, 'Work and money', begins with a
recent photograph carrying the caption 'Cleaning salmon at B.C. Packers' and
follows this with the reminiscences of Moto Suzuki, a retired cannery worker.
The visual image shows concentrated activity and distinguishes clearly between
the women at their task (a row, endless it would seem, of intent faces, turbaned

heads, white overalls, gloved hands) and the hectic carcases of salmon in a deep trough of water. If we have any feelings for the torn and plundered fish, these are liable to be tempered with consideration for the welfare of the workers since, from Suzuki's comments, things might be worse. As it is, compared to the 1920s, there is more work these days, more money all round.

From beneath the pilings, however, another perspective emerges. This improved quality of life is linked to the death-dealing 'trucks of production', the impersonal system of big corporations that harness natural instincts to the service of profit. Salmon which return to the same river to spawn, human beings with few aspirations other than making a sort of life for themselves – all are determined by their place in production. If in the course of *Steveston* Marlatt gives weight to the experiences of women, this is due in part to her attempt to redress the predominantly male view of history in *Steveston Recollected*. (Only two of the ten central figures interviewed are women.) In part it is that women, especially those in the canneries, are doubly disadvantaged, 'lockt into menstrual cycles, into pregnancy, childbirth' as well as taxing work.[8] Themselves the 'slaves of the canneries', their children too are in pawn on account of the debts owed for food, housing, boats, fishing gear. 'Imperial Cannery 1913' registers the expanding consciousness of a growing girl, eager to move forward into adulthood yet wary of the grim realities into which she will be sucked.

> Now she is old enough to be her
> mother inside, working, with the smallest one standing by her skirt
> in grubby dress, & the blood streams down the wooden cutting board
> as the 'iron chink' (that's what they call it) beheads each fish

In these lines enacting the repetitive rhythms of work and of existence, salmon, girl and woman ('her', 'her mother', 'fish') are bound by their positioning in the text, their place in production, their fertility ('the blood streams').

Yet even the 'iron chink' must seem antiquated and droll when set against modern day techniques of salmon canning. In 'Steveston as you find it',

> It's wet,
> & there's a fish smell. There's a subhuman, sub/marine aura to things. The
> cavernous 'fresh fish' shed filled with water, with wet bodies of dead fish
> in thousands, wet aprons & gloves of warm bodies whose hands expertly
> trim, cut, fillet, pack these bodies reduced to non-bodies, nonsensate food
> *these* bodies ache from, feet in gumboots on wet cement, arms moving,
> hands, cold blowing in from open doors facing the river, whose ears dull
> from, the insensate noise of machinery, of forklifts, of grinding & washing,
> of conveyor belt. Put on an extra sweater, wear long underwear against
> the damp that creeps up from this asphalt, from this death that must be
> kept cool, fresh.

The impact of this carnage derives from, among other things, the images of dismemberment (arms, hands, ears); the ambiguities of words like 'subhuman' (lower than human beings on the evolutionary scale? reduced on account of the numbing work to something less than human? morally degraded?); the toilsome repetitions of 'bodies' within an eliding syntax so that fish and humans, wet bodies and warm ones, are reduced indistinguishably to 'non-bodies' and then, rhyming insidiously with 'fresh' some lines later, simply 'flesh'.

Belonging becomes synonymous with entrapment, progress with death. The irony is the more bitter in those instances where, owing to the powerful influence of the corporations and the efficacy of his own skills, the exploited victim ends up an adherent of the system of profit and big business.

> Were you fined? Did you cross the border
> inadvertently. Did chart & compass, all direction, fail? Interned,
> your people confined to a small space where rebirth, will,
> push you out thru the rings of material prosperity at war's
> end fixed, finally, as citizens of an exploited earth:
> you drive your own car, construct your own house, create your
> registered place at Packers' camp, walk the fine (concrete)
> line of private property.

The narrative movement of *Steveston Recollected* is retraced here but with a strong suggestion of the circle closing in on itself. 'Finally' is weighed down with negative overtones of finality, 'fine' comes up against its own irony, and journeys of quest ('did chart and compass, all direction, fail?') lead to little more than the circumscribed satisfactions of private property. The once enduring myths of return, among them the *Odyssey*, the visitations of Persephone, 'the winter ceremonial' of the Kwakiutl Indians, appear to have atrophied. Only boredom awaits Ulysses, the 'concrete' of housing developments and the 'oily ring' of pollution greet the daughter of earth, and an unregenerate society fails to tame the madness of the *hamatsa*, his hunger for human flesh.[9]

So far my reading of *Steveston* has emphasized the disasters, the death. To insist upon such a reading, however, is to replace one version of Steveston's story with another, an arbitrary act when language and form in Marlatt's poetry are given over to a ceaseless striving for fullness of vision.

> Always there is this shadow, long, that underlies the street & twins it,
> running it to ground. As the river, at Atlas camp, throws up sand that cuts
> the line Moncton extends (in mind) to the end. A line that lies, like
> Moncton straight ahead, ignores this shadow that wavers & wanders,
> collecting islands of lives, leaves them stranded or suddenly, after some
> years visible as, time passing, picking stucco off the wall outside Hiro's, or
> drinking pop & trading bubblegum cards. It lengthens slowly . . . . . . . .

In this passage, for example, ominous though 'this shadow' may be in harking back to 'the shadow of charred stilts', it has a vitality and subtlety which make themselves felt in the press of verbs, the half-rhymes that hover and move on, the delicate wordplay. It 'underlies' (underlines), 'twins' (twines), runs (with) the street (down) to the ground and, having reached that limit ('ground' – earth, bottom of sea), comes back transformed into river ('as' – in the role of), a line of verse ('the line that lies'), 'time passing', a growing generation, the salmon's seaward course. In that push outwards followed by the return, and then the swing outwards again, is expressed the interaction of river and sea, the natural instincts of the salmon, and the dynamics of Marlatt's long poem, refusing closure, transcending cyclicality.

In one of her cogitations about form, Marlatt describes this spiralling as 'still moving towards some recognition',[10] some means, that is, of knowing again. Consequently, once stated, ideas and motifs in *Steveston* return and are remade. Coming after 'In Time', 'Work' picks up on 'twin[n]ing', recasting the theme in terms of a human encounter. Meeting in Christine's cafe, the I narrator and the fisherman are teased by their curiosity about each other. But her deft sketches and comments as an interviewer only impinge upon his public self, leaving her baffled by the 'invisibility that stalks beside him'. Which is the real person? Expert fisherman? embittered prisoner of war? respectable head of family? old lecher? heroic seafarer? astute business man? bored layabout? As his voice intrudes into her narrative, its different registers (cajolery, matter of factness, casual propositions, self-irony) intimate the many sides of his reality and, at the same time, his perplexed constructions of her variety – hippie, sexual object, serious researcher, busybody, easy prey, the unknown. In each case, once the possibilities begin to multiply, the neat structures and solid certainties of the early part of the poem are eroded, leaving words vaguely gesturing and verse paragraphs adrift.

But still, his hand pushing
down there, the teasing smile, 'Next time I fish West Coast I take you
with me eh?' that persists, that isn't meant to tease but to imply . . .
No, it's an old
dream my hair, my body happens to fit: the incarnate goal of all
that's *out there*, given birth in crowded ghetto conditions,
necessity to work up out of that mass, the pressure always ('after
the war they wouldn't even rent a house to us') to feel what one
man can do, where he can go . . .

And yet it is in the helplessness precisely – 'all that's *out there*' – that the 'recognition', the knowing again, is located and self and other momentarily connect.

Set against this the conflicting desire of the immigrant consciousness for the 'deepest sense' of Steveston 'here now & myself here now in it',[11] and it is no longer the *nisei*, bound as they are to the traumas of the past and the psychological compensations which economic power brings, to whom Marlatt must turn.

'I'm not really in
the Japanese community, I don't belong to Buddhist Church, I don't
send my kids to sunday school.'

The voice that is heard in 'Or there is love', the poem leading out of 'Ghost', springs from the next generation. Casting aside formal allegiances, the elusive presence figured there takes instead to the natural environment; making her home at the edge, at the intersection of land, river, sea, she finds common ground with salmon and fox; mindful of the 'empty dykes & misplaced hope' of her forebears, she gathers herself in to the secret resources of the terrain. The constituting experience of the poem is this journeying towards an awareness of self and its full functioning in the course of which conventional categories of perception ('in here'/'out there', external reality/inner truth, space/place, the mundane/the significant, word/action) break down and reality 'confuses' (from Latin, *confusus*) with rich mingling.

> And coming from town, driving down by the scummy & soontobecovered
> ditches (remnant, of leftover rains, plucked cabbages in the sun, & wind)
> where do you find her, out?
>             as now by day,
>                       or in, summer's wilder growth, around &
> past (the stepping stones at back are wood and cut by hand) amidst (there is
> no closer) hands full of beans & fingers in the heart of, 'well I *live* here',
> lettuce, children, friends, you find a self, under the trees that sway like
> underwater weeds, connecting things.

In these lines, as elsewhere, strategies of ordering cannot be separated from those of displacement as Marlatt speaks this 'lived world',[12] drawing exuberantly and inventively from her poetic talents which include a precise and unerring craftsmanship, an extraordinary sensitivity to the resonances of language and a play of mind thoroughly attuned to multiplicity. Aptly 'connecting things' marks a point of arrival which is also one of departure. Positioned at what would have been midway in a line of sixteen syllables, and corresponding thereby with 'you find a self' in the line immediately above, it attracts that phrase to itself producing a single statement in which the action of 'connecting' is attributed to 'a self', an agent of consciousness. Add to this statement 'under the trees' and it satisfies the earlier, punning inquiry with answers both to her location ('where do you find her?') and her inner person ('where do you find her out?'). This syntactically coherent reading, from left to right of the lines and down the page, is only one, however, of a plurality of readings which the text generates and which, running alongside and counter, call into question its stability.

Consider 'connecting things' as an adjectival phrase instead of a verb phrase and one unusual feature of the passage is highlighted, which is the nervous activity accruing to words classed as 'closed' grammatical items, for example, articles, conjunctions, pronouns, prepositions.[13] Thus in the phrase 'you find a self', the throwaway 'a', by echoing 'your' and 'her', collapses from within the distinctions between reader, character, narrator. Furthermore, reading back across the whole passage finds this self(s) all-pervasive, 'under the trees' and also 'in the heart of' things (or her hands and fingers are), 'in', 'around' and 'past' 'summer's wilder growth', or simply 'in', 'around', and (gone) 'past'. Lastly, the undefined grammatical status of the pivotal 'like' in 'under the trees that sway like/underwater weeds' means that it is continually shifting layers of meaning. As an adverb, 'like' points attention to 'sway' (the trees move in that manner, 'as it were'); as a conjunction, to the similarity in movement between the trees and the weeds (the trees sway in the manner the weeds sway); as a preposition, and with 'underwater' split into two words, to similar selves in different situations (the self under the trees is like the one under the weeds).[14]

In these instances, 'connecting things' (as action and object) brings one into touch with multitude and mystery, and nowhere more hauntingly than in the last instance when, quiet and secretive, the salmon is conjured from its retreat. Like the 'self' in 'Or there is love', it belongs to Steveston the place. Like the poet who inhabits the narrative of her own work, it is intrinsic to *Steveston*, the long poem. The basis of life and material wealth, it also proliferates meaning as the symbol of death, rebirth, fertility, chance, timelessness, the ephemeral moment. Its energies galvanize the town's existence and shape the narrative. Its presence is located in place, in the poem's parts, and is also out there, interpenetrating the whole.

In *Touch to My Tongue*, Marlatt alludes to 'these endless similes, this continuing fascination with making one out of two, a new one, a simultitude'.[15] The neologism is noted by Laurie Ricou in investigating the principles of female discourse and, choosing to focus upon the criterion of dissimilarity rather than of resemblance inherent in similes, he comments felicitously on the way the word 'tricks the eye with similitude and hides a multitude'.[16] From my reading of *Steveston*, I am prompted myself to highlight the notion of 'simultaneity'[17] which, incorporated in 'simultitude', enables it thereby to hold 'multitude' in its grasp as one, and as many all at once. For it seems to me that only by returning to the originating impulse behind similes and metaphors, that is, the desire to produce pleasure and significance by conveying, in the same instance, likeness and difference,[18] is it possible to identify a poetics which will encompass the problem central to *Steveston* – 'the rift of language, race, & sex' ('End of Cannery Channel') within a predominantly immigrant community. Finally, a strong persuasion of the impossibility of a critic's task as well as its fascination has dictated the title of this essay. In calling it 'One Cast of a Net', I have in mind also the useful information delivered by one of the fishermen in *Steveston Recollected*: 'there are different sizes of mesh for different fish, different shades of green, too, for varying depths of water'.[19] I offer the title therefore as intending only one way of reading Daphne Marlatt's rich and complex poem.

### Notes

1 Daphne Marlatt, interviewed by George Bowering in 'Given This Body', *Open Letter*, 4th series, 3, Spring 1979, p. 35.

2 'Entering In: The Immigrant Imagination', in W.H. New (ed.), *Canadian Writers of 1984*, Vancouver, University of British Columbia Press, 1984, p. 220.

3 W.G. Beasley, *Japanese Imperialism 1894–1945*, Oxford, Clarendon Press, 1987.

4 Daphne Marlatt (ed.), 'Introduction', *Steveston Recollected: A Japanese–Canadian History*, Victoria, Provincial Archives of British Columbia, 1975, p. xiii.

5 The work, with photographs by Robert Minden, was published in 1974 by Talonbooks, Vancouver. *Steveston Recollected*, held up for a while by lack of funds, was published later, in 1975.

6 Dorothy Livesay, 'The Documentary Poem: A Canadian Genre', in Eli Mandel (ed.), *Contexts of Canadian Criticism*, Chicago, Chicago University Press, 1971, p. 267.

7 Frank Davey, 'Countertextuality in the Long Poem', in *Open Letter*, 6th Series, 2–3, Summer-Fall 1985, pp. 36–41.

8 'Given This Body', p. 73.

9 For a concise account of the Kwakiutl world and worldview, see John Bentley Mays, 'Ariadne: Prolegomenon to the Poetry of Daphne Marlatt', in *Open Letter*, 3rd Series, 3, Fall 1975, pp. 23–9.

10 Daphne Marlatt, *What Matters: Writing 1968–70*, Toronto, Coach House Press, 1980), p. 71.

11 Entry under 'Daphne Marlatt', in 'Statements by the Poets', in Michael Ondaatje (ed.), *The Long Poem Anthology*, Toronto, Coach House Press, 1979, p. 316.

12 See Douglas Barbour, 'The Phenomenological I: Daphne Marlatt's *Steveston*', in Diane Bessai and David Jackel (eds), *Figures in a Ground*, Saskatoon, Western Producer Prairie Books, 1978.

13 Entry under 'closed (1)', in David Crystal, *A Dictionary of Linguistics and Phonetics,*: Oxford, Blackwell, 1985, p. 51.

14 The following is one of many delightful illustrations of human intimacy with the natural world occurring in James P. Spradley, *Guests Never Leave Hungry: The Autobiography of James Sewid, A Kwakiutl Indian*, New Haven, Yale, University Press, 1969, p. 22: 'I used to enjoy swimming among the fish when they were spawning. I guess that's the reason why I love fish. I would like to live among the fish as long as I live.'

15 'Musing with Mothertongue', in *Touch to My Tongue*, Edmonton, Longspoon Press, 1984, p. 46.

16 'Phyllis Webb, Daphne Marlatt and simultitude', in *A Mazing Space: Writing Canadian Women Writing*, Edmonton, Longspoon Press, 1986, p. 215.

17 Cf. Marlatt's comment in *What Matters*, p. 70: 'the *simultaneity* of experience (so many elements occurring in consciousness at once) – the rapidity of conscious movement (of what appears in "lime light" – one thought leading to the next – or being called up by the preceding – it is not a linear extension but much more a spiralling . . .'

18 I am indebted here to I.A. Richards, *The Philosophy of Rhetoric*, London, Oxford University Press, 1971 and to the fine explication of this work in Paul Ricoeur, *The Rule of Metaphor*, London, Routledge, 1978.

19 *Steveston Recollected*, p. 1.

# 7

# On Gender and Writing: Marian Engel's *Bear* and *The Tattooed Woman*

## Coral Ann Howells

Ordinary reality keeps turning on me. What I have to deal with is super-reality, that element in everyday life where the surreal shows itself without turning French on us.

Introduction to *The Tattooed Woman*[1]

In his preface to Marian Engel's posthumously published collection of short stories in *The Tattooed Woman* (1985) Timothy Findley describes them as having a kind of 'collective oddness'. His remark not only underlines her own comments but is itself remarkably at odds with William French's assessment of Engel in the *Globe and Mail* obituary (18 February 1985) where he describes her as

delineating the plight of contemporary women with uncommon perception . . . Her viewpoint was not that of the militant feminist; she was concerned with the grubbiness and grittiness of everyday existence, and the small acts of heroism that enabled her heroines to survive with dignity.

While French's praise calls attention to the character interest and realism of Engel's fiction, it would seem that the very survival procedures of her heroines involve strategies of displacement which 'turn French' on French, for these stories are characterized not by their realism but by their frequent slippages away from everyday existence into dimensions of fantasy. It is with the shifts in narrative between realism and fantasy that I am concerned in this discussion of Engel's best known novel, *Bear* (1976), and three of the stories in *The Tattooed Woman*, for such shiftiness argues for Engel's positive relation to the doubled discourse of feminist writing in a way that French's obituary ignores or disallows.

My essay title, with its acknowledgement to Michelene Wandor's collection of women writers' essays, signals the feminist critical context within which Engel's 'oddness' may be read, not only as personal idiosyncracy but also as deliberately feminist textual strategy.[2] While her viewpoint may not have been that of a militant feminist, her fiction shows a keen awareness of sexual positioning and its effect on women's writing, with its insistent challenging of literary conventions and the equally insistent self-criticism of her female protagonists. Engel's writing would seem a vividly particular illustration of women's ambivalent relation to cultural and literary traditions and their attempts to revise these traditions in order to accommodate the feminine angle on experience. As feminist critics have pointed out, women writers claim their textual space by disruptive tactics, subverting conventions of realism by shifts into fantasy or romance, by mixing genres so that one code is superimposed upon another. Through such split-level discourse they create a doubled vision which is also a characteristically feminine entertainment of simultaneous alternatives. This is exactly Engel's method in *Bear*, with its breaking down of genre boundaries between pastoral, pornography and myth as she revises Canadian wilderness narratives through the mode of female sexual fantasy. It is also the method of the short stories where realistic narratives are undermined by their mixture of genre codes, so that (as Engel says in her introduction, p. xi), 'The skin of logic is pulled back [and] anything can happen.'

Both the novel and the stories are dominated by a sense of loss and mortality, telling the truth about waning flesh in their recognition of what ageing means physically for a woman; yet they are also double faced in their exploration of possible ways of transcending limits of the body through imagination and through art. We may agree with William French on one point when he praises Engel's 'delineation of the plight of contemporary women' if by that he means her registration of women's fragmented experience of writing and identity. Cora Kaplan's excellent essay in Wandor's collection, while identifying fragmentation as the characteristic of all human subjectivity, gives her argument a feminist slant by claiming that a 'will-full, unified and cohered subject' is only a fiction, and that the woman's perspective revises an outdated male romantic ideology: 'Romantic ideologies of the subject suppress this crucial and potentially hopeful incoherence, or make its absence a sign of weakness and thus an occasion for mourning or reparation.'[3] Kaplan argues in favour of a feminist politics which 'will no longer overvalue control, rationality and individual power, and which instead, tries to understand human desire, struggle and agency as they are mobilised through a more complicated, less finished and less heroic psychic schema' (p. 59). It is in such a context that Engel's stories of women's sense of their own insufficiency take on a new dimension, for her split-level discourse invents a breathing space for her protagonists to relate to lost selves or fantasy images, to see beyond culturally determined representations of the feminine. Her texts provide temporarily the impossible spaces of desire.

*Bear* confronts what one Canadian feminist describes as 'the dominant cultural discourse and its male point of view which denies female sexuality'[4] by working explicitly within the genre of male pornographic fantasy, but telling the story from the woman's point of view where the Other is no longer female but male.[5] Interestingly, when Engel enters on this forbidden territory she displays a certain defiance (and defensiveness?) by inventing a scenario which is almost parodic: the male is not a human but a bear. Such figuring is a witty conflation of sexual and wilderness fantasies, where Lou, the well read Toronto archivist, sees herself as the inheritor of male traditions which she proceeds to revise. Thinking of Beau Brummel and Colonel Cary who was Byron's contemporary and the 'landscape nut' who had settled in the Canadian bush,

> She felt victorious over them; she felt she was their inheritor; a woman
> rubbing her foot in the thick black pelt of a bear was more than they
> would have imagined. More, too, than a military victory: splendour.[6]

What Lou inherits are male romantic dreams of wilderness and self-transcendence, but her dream has a characteristically female inflection. It is neither imperialist, isolationist nor imported like the first Colonel Cary's, but strongly affective in its unattainable dreams of intimate contact with the wilderness. The way to transcendence as she sees it is through love – sexual love for a wilderness creature – for Lou's fantasy of desire transgresses limits to the point of taboo. As sexual fantasy it involves transformations of the beloved object in the eyes of the gazer (and the bear is her ideal object, malleable to her imagination yet ultimately unknowable) just as it re-enacts traditional patterns of submission and violation (cf. Alice Munro, 'I can't apologize for the banality of my dreams').[7] However, there is a difference here for it is the woman who is initiator and agent and the bear which 'served her' (p. 118) in her sexual pleasure. Yet as Alice Munro so wisely tells us about the same area of experience, 'The images, the language of pornography and romance are alike: monotonous and mechanically seductive, quickly leading to despair' ('Bardon Bus', p. 123). They also lead to the recognition of impossibility, as Lou discovers when she tries to copulate with the bear (p. 131):

> She took her sweater off and went down on all fours in front of him, in the
> animal posture. He reached out one great paw and ripped the skin on her
> back.

It is the bear's action which scarifies her into a sense of herself as human, of him as animal, and of the inviolability of the natural order. That encounter spells the end of her fantasy of the 'high whistling communion that had bound them during the summer' (p. 134).

By the end we realize that the novel was constructed on this recognition of impossibility, for Lou's erotic wilderness fantasy is enacted within a very civilized context, in Colonel Cary's artificially constructed pastoral retreat; it is also aided and abetted by his books and his handwritten notes about bear legends, as she continues to pursue her professional assignment for the Toronto Historical Institute. Fantasies of transcendence/transgression are enacted within enclosed spaces, the limits of which have already been prescribed, just as the places of the woman and the bear are predetermined.

This is the fantasy of a lonely woman, invented to heal loss, to 'heal guilt' (p. 140), offering only a glimpse of forbidden communion with the wilderness, climaxed in a moment when Lou's self-enclosing skin is torn open. This unlooked for moment brings panic and terror, though it is succeeded by a deep sleep which releases her into a rehabilitated view of herself (pp. 133–4):

> [She] looked at herself naked in the great oval pier-glass once more. She was different. She seemed to have the body of a much younger woman . . . Slowly she turned and looked over her shoulder in the pier-glass at her back: one long, red, congealing weal marked her from shoulder to buttock. I shall keep that, she thought. And it is not the mark of Cain.

The novel ends not as fantasy nor as realistic discourse, but with a mixture of the two in the final consoling image of the Great Bear constellation, which Lou sees while driving back to Toronto: 'It was a brilliant night, all star-shine, and overhead the Great Bear and his thirty-seven thousand virgins kept her company' (p. 141). Sexual longing is transformed by the light of the stars into a vision which is close to mystical communion. The stars may be 'always out of reach' (p. 122), but they are still there.

Experience leaves its marks less benignly in *The Tattooed Woman*, for in these stories of middle age ('Instant War Memorials', as Engel calls them in her introduction, p. xi) it is the condition of the walking wounded that provides the narrative framework. Though in this collection there is no formal unity of character recurrence or referential framework of place, and though ten of the sixteen stories have been published previously over the ten-year period since 1975, there are strong unifying factors which result in the 'collective oddness' that Findley noted. There is continuity in the recurrent thematic motif of the double in these stories of secret lives, where doubling spells both the recognition of disparities and the effort to make connections between them. There is also a collective oddness of narrative method, where every story highlights the discontinuities between realism and fantasy as different kinds of discourse. 'Could I Have Found a Better Love Than You?' is the most dazzling example in this collection of the interplay of signals from one literary code against another, where the language of a gardening catalogue provides a framework for the shifts between realism and myth. Just as the language of the catalogue opens up imaginative spaces in the text, so writing itself assumes the power to transform ordinariness. This may be through the process of fiction making as in 'Gemini, Gemino' or through the very act of writing, as in the title story where a woman writes on her own skin. It is a bizarre form of writing not unlike the savage writing of the bear's claw slashing the woman's back in *Bear*, and in both cases the inscriptions have the power of primitive magic. Though I do not see

Engel as a Canadian practitioner of 'magic realism' in the mode of Jack Hodgins or Graeme Gibson, it would seem that in these stories reality is being transformed through the magic of writing. The conventions of realism split to reveal glimpses of the incongruities within reality, which gives the collection its distinctive oddness and a kind of unity in its insistent attention to disunities.

The title story signals its oddity from the beginning. As Findley remarks, 'A person does not, as a rule, for instance, decide to draw attention to herself when she feels her husband leaving her, by scarring herself with razor blades' (p. viii). But that is exactly what happens here. This is a story about a forty-two-year-old woman whose husband tells her that he is having an affair with a young woman who works in his drugstore. What the wife does in response to this is to go down to the shopping plaza and sit behind a fern watching the two of them on the closed circuit television he had installed 'to prevent thievery', and in the evening she starts carving signs on her body with a razor blade – stars and curvy lines and crosshatchings of little houses and trees. When her husband finds out he sends her to a psychiatrist, though he does not come back to her and she is left alone. That story could have been called *Bodily Harm*, but then it would have blurred the central image of the woman with signs written on her flesh. The narrative is important only to give readers evidence to decode those signs and it leads back to the signs at the end with the psychiatrist's remark, 'You should go somewhere hot. It will make a very striking tan' (p. 9).

These incisions are another form of a woman's writing – her 'tattooing' – is a story within a story using pictographs instead of words. If autobiographical writing is a textual presentation of the self, what history of the self is being presented here to be deciphered? These signs are a challenge, demanding to be looked at and read. It seems that the only thing the woman knows she possesses is her own body which her husband has rejected in favour of the girl's. It is only on her body that she can register the emotional harm done to her, and she works in the only medium that she and her husband have ever valued. Seeing herself as a physical object, she tries by her carving to transform a useless object into an art object (p. 8):

> I'm an artist now, she thought, a true artist. My body is my canvas. I am very old and very beautiful. I am carved like an old shaman. I am an artifact of an old culture . . . My body has been used and bent and violated and broken, but I have resisted. I am Somebody.

We may see the woman's writing as fetish, but to see it only as self-mutilation would be a reductive outside view. Yet the questions remain. How close do we as readers ever get to the inside view and how much does the woman herself understand it?[8]

As a mode of response this woman's effort parallels to a remarkable degree the comments made by Susan Gubar in her essay, 'The Blank Page and the Issues of Female Creativity':

Many women experience their own bodies as the only available medium for their art, with the result that the distance between the woman artist and her art is often radically diminished; second, one of the primary and most resonant metaphors provided by the female body is blood, and cultural forms of creativity are often experienced as a painful wounding.[9]

There are many examples in literature of women or female bodies being described as canvases or blank sheets to be written on by experience. Gubar's essay cites examples from James and Conrad, to which we may add Hardy's Tess and the image of the virgin page, the passive object waiting to be inscribed. There is also Maxine Hong Kingston's Woman Warrior who goes into battle scarred with the legends of her culture written all over her back. There is Lou's naked back on which the bear writes the demarcation line between humanness and bestiality. However in 'The Tattooed Woman' the woman does the writing herself. Someone who has always been self-effacing now draws attention to her body. Why does she do this? She says she does it out of love, and her analyst suggests that it is a form of mourning for the loss of her husband; but is it not likely that she really writes on herself out of rage? This is her act of rebellion, a fantastic self-assertion through which she transforms herself into 'a wise old woman'. As both artist and artefact she has redefined herself out of being a good wife into being 'Somebody.' She both does and does not follow the rules of her culture. Indeed she concentrates on her face, but instead of following the conventions of make up she subverts those rules as she cuts stars into her forehead. It is a disfigurement which is a refiguring, where what is suppressed is given visible form, for as she reasons, 'Experience must show' (p. 6).

This woman is inarticulate; she cannot tell the story of her love, her loss, her rage, but she experiences it directly in her body and writes it in code on her skin. There is nothing original about the signs: the trees and houses would appear to signify the woman's domestic history and the stars have a parallel in *Bear* where they are signs of aspiration, though 'always out of reach'. This combination images the oppositions between the woman's enclosed life (inside the home, inside her marriage, in the indoor shopping plaza) and her desire for travel and for the openness of sunshine and heat. There seems to be a subterranean connection here between the African statues of D.H. Lawrence's *Women in Love* and what the African women in the *National Geographics* represent for this woman.[10] She will make her rejected body beautiful as it becomes the medium for her creativity and the visible sign of her aspiration towards wisdom. The analyst acts as interpreter for the woman and for the reader. While she offers inadequate readings of her own writing, it is the analyst who sees that the tattooing is an attempt to proclaim herself and her history. Perhaps this is why the story ends by highlighting the tattooed woman image in the advice to get a suntan so that the hidden experiences will show on the surface. However, the ending leaves us faintly uneasy: it is too close to Engel's characteristic ironical quips which repress as much as they reveal (cf. the ending of 'Gemini, Gemino'). What might also be seen to be revealed are an individual woman's pain and her hankerings after transcendence.

While 'The Tattooed Woman' has the shape of a modernist short story, with its moment of clarification at the end, and told like Joyce's *Dubliners* in a style of 'scrupulous meanness', 'Could I Have Found a Better Love than You? Notes on the Life of Miss Iris Terryberry with Excerpts from the Terryberry Garden Perennial Catalogue' has the shape of a postmodernist narrative with its multiple voices and fragmented structure. Told in the first person by a middle-aged female narrator, the narrative is disrupted from time to time by entries quoted from the Terryberry garden catalogue. The method is analogous to Robert Kroetsch's poem 'Seed Catalogue' (1977), taking quotations from one kind of text and inserting them into the context of another so that they are the same in form but different in function. This incorporation of vestiges from the past is, as Kroetsch describes it, an archaeological method allowing for discontinuity, layering and imaginative speculation.[11] It is also a clear demonstration of the mixing of genre codes, where a narrative of women in reduced circumstances ('We aren't what we were', p. 144) is supplemented by a different discourse giving glimpses into a vanished romantic world and forging connections with the past. The effect is what Del Jordan in *Lives of Girls and Women* would call 'a solid intrusion of the legendary into the real world', and itself constitutes a reason for the narrator's comment, 'It makes me boil with anger when people say Canadians have no history' (p. 144).

The story interweaves the contrasting worlds of conventional small town Western Ontario and Miss Iris Terryberry's secret alternative world which is enclosed in her catalogue. That is a glamorous world of chorus girls and aristocrats, ruffles, pale velvet, silver shimmers and luxuriant bloom. The descriptions of the plants are themselves a hybrid mixture of codes with their *fin de siècle* imagery and their modest commercialism (p. 143):

Terryberry's Favourite: Rich mauve standards, flamboyant violet falls, heavily ruffled and gartered in purple. Try a cluster of chorus girls at your door. Mid-season, $4 and worth it.

Such exoticism is Miss Terryberry's way of transcending a very limited life, for her flowers (as artificially created as the carnations and streaked gillyvors in *The Winter's Tale*) are frequently named after her friends and relatives whom she transforms by the benign magic of her imagination into strange romantic beings. When the narrator's husband visits Miss Terryberry he thinks she is a witch who works magic spells; his intuition is right. He also sees the drawings of flowers made by her nephew Cordell and his comment is revealing (p. 152):

You couldn't say the drawings were bad, they were a world, they drew me in, they scared hell out of me. I mean at first they just looked like flowers and then I realised they were, well – perverse.

Cordell has already been transformed in name and substance by Miss Terryberry into Della Robbia (p. 153):

> Della Robbia: Gorgeous pale pink, green at the heart, shading to violet at petal's edge. White veins and stamens, green anthers. Loose, floating form, luxuriant bloom, exotic for a Canadian heterocallis.

As Miss Terryberry's familiar he is the heir to her witchcraft and her precious Chinese peonies which she gives to him when she knows she is going to die.

In the course of the story Miss Terryberry's exotic world of flowers gradually becomes the dark territory of death and myth which the narrator can glimpse but where she cannot follow: 'I had a vision of Della at the mouth of Hades, blue torch of peony in his hand. Was it joy or terror on his face?' (p. 154). The non-human world of plants with its elemental energy and cycles of birth, decay and death becomes the mythic realm of the classical underworld. The method is not unlike that of D. H. Lawrence's poem 'Bavarian Gentians' where the separate worlds of human and non-human are juxtaposed and fused.

Miss Terryberry's funeral and her two obituaries continue to weave the delicate web of connections between everyday decorum and the underground world of hidden natural processes which borders on the dark world of myth. The *Canadian Plant Breeder's Journal* obituary is itself an intriguing mixture of codes, signalling myth and then recuperating its strangeness in the language of conventional elegy (p. 154):

> The Herbaceous Peony Cerberus: A deep maroon with golden stamens, shaggy and rich in form, was perhaps Miss Terryberry's most luxurious contribution to the Canadian garden, though the Terry series of iris cannot be faulted for purity of colour and richness of bloom, and she had a pleasant taste in daylilies. Her output was small – she refused to expand although there were several opportunities – and the select varieties she chose to work with responded almost lovingly to her touch. Whether you went to her for luscious Ellen Terry peonies, Terrylime-and-lemon iris, or a basket of pansies and pinks, you felt privileged to be a customer. The old order changeth, there will not be another like her.

It is the narrator's private obituary at the end that is Miss Terryberry's true portrait (p. 155):

> Louisa's Favourite: A lean brown daylily, meagre-blooming, unruffled, but with golden stamens and strange, silver veins. Dignified, but merry in the breeze; unpredictable: not like anything else you have ever seen.

Miss Terryberry's catalogue is her challenge to the ordinary world, giving a glimpse of the magic and mystery which the world lacks. The coded narratives of her and Louisa are complementary, separate but inseparable as they present the coexistence of the everyday and the mythic. The dying Miss Terryberry is an eccentric guide. As she tells Louisa in her unpretentiously double language,

'You keep your yellows and your purples segregated and you get back to Eden where colours ran true' (p. 147). I cannot escape the haunting suggestion here that a way back to Eden is suggested but that it is a way that leads through death and the underworld – which may give readers a tremor when we remember that Engel wrote this story while she was dying of cancer.[12]

In the final story 'Gemini, Gemino' many of the distinctive features of this collection swing into focus: the doubles theme which is written into its title, the resurrection of a hidden past, death, and the double faced function of writing itself. The protagonists are another middle-aged married couple, a male novelist and his wife (p. 181):

> He was a decent man, a fair husband, and a good writer. He knew that.
> He had seen these statements written in the newspapers and written on
> his heart. And his wife lay weeping on the sand.

A story about the difficulties of novel writing and novel reading, it is told from two points of view where the duplicitous nature of fiction generates the tension between the man and the woman. While he emphasizes the discontinuities between fiction and real life his wife asserts, 'You can't blame me for reading it from my point of view', registering the shock of connections with her own past and asserting the falsity of his fictional creation. The collision between points of view forms the substance of this story, throwing up unforeseen parallels as well as differences between husband and wife. His novel about twin sisters has revealed to them both their isolation, their childhood damaging, their vulnerabilities, but no benison is offered as it was in the earlier story 'The Confession Tree'. Instead, in its exposure of secret lives the novel has become a form of betrayal. As his wife says, 'If you sell me, sell me well.' And her husband does (p. 192):

> The book's very intensity brought it a small, Canadian and respectable
> kind of fame. It earned prestigious reviews in England but was too low-
> key for the Americans. Joan took up yoga and left him alone more than
> ever. He committed untold extravagances with the Garden Club cata-
> logue, refused to appear on psychological panels about twins, and lived in
> fear and hope of meeting a beautiful fair woman who was blind.

It is a wry ending to a story about the dangers of taking life (someone else's life) and transforming it into fiction.

Writing, be it a novel or a short story or a garden catalogue or making marks on a body, is a dangerous occupation. The narrative forms may differ, but the very process of transforming real life into writing subverts the mimetic function of realism, opening up cracks in the surface through which the underworld of suppressed rage and desire or fears of failure and death break through into visibility. About her fiction making Engel said (introduction, p. xiii):

> More and more, the irrational, the magical impulse, dominates my work.
> When the mirror cracks I find the compression necessary to miniaturize

the narrative drawl, create a world in small compass ... If the parts persist in going their own way, gulping down huge drafts of time, I have the outline of a novel on my hands.

Her emphasis is on writing as invention not as imitation; fictionality begins 'when the mirror cracks'. *Bear* and the stories in *The Tattooed Woman* draw attention to writing and to the different codes that characters may use for their story telling. They also highlight the creative functioning of language (or of more primitive sign systems) as a way to transcend, however ambiguously, the limitations of the characters' shrunken lives. What Findley calls Engel's 'odd-ness' results from the narrative shifts between ordinariness and those moments when 'the skin of logic is pulled back [and] anything can happen'. Realism, like everyday life, needs to be supplemented by elements of the irrational, the magical, the mythical; and it is with the interweaving of these codes that Engel manages to invent fictions which look as if they reflect the surfaces of ordinary reality but which also peer through to the other side of the looking glass through the cracks in the mirror. 'Sure, they're women's books, because they're about women and written by a woman ... Who's afraid of women's books? [13]

## Notes

1  M. Engel, *The Tattooed Woman*, Harmondsworth, Penguin, 1985, p. xiii. Quota-tions are from this edition.
2  Relevant feminist criticism includes Michelene Wandor (ed.), *On Gender and Writing*, London, Pandora, 1983; Toril Moi, *Sexual/Textual Politics: Feminist Literary Theory*, London, Methuen, 1985; S. Neuman and S. Kamboureli (eds), *A Mazing Space: Writing Canadian Women Writing*, Edmonton, NeWest, 1986.
3  C. Kaplan, 'Speaking/Writing/Feminism', *On Gender and Writing*, pp. 51–61.
4  S. Neuman, 'Importing Difference: Feminist Theory and Canadian Women Writers', *A Mazing Space*, pp. 392–405 and J. Moss (ed.), *Future Indicative: Literary Theory and Canadian Literature*, University of Ottawa Press, 1987, pp. 95–116.
5  I have written about *Bear* in *Private and Fictional Words*, London, Methuen, 1987, pp. 108–18, so this section is really a continuation of my earlier reading of the novel.
6  M. Engel, *Bear*, Toronto, McClelland and Stewart, New Canadian Library, 1982, p. 52. Quotations are from this edition.
7  A. Munro, 'Bardon Bus', *The Moons of Jupiter*, Toronto, Macmillan, 1982 p. 127.
8  Women's self-mutilation is a most complicated issue, as Elizabeth Ikiru's memoir of her mental illness confirms, where such behaviour is evidently a form of self hatred and self-punishment (*Saturday Night*, April 1985), pp. 30–9.
9  S. Gubar, 'The Blank Page and the Issues of Female Creativity', in E. Abel (ed.), *Writing and Sexual Difference*, Brighton, Harvester, 1982, pp. 73–93.
10  In interview with Carroll Klein, Engel speaks of her enthusiasm for D. H. Lawrence (*Room on One's Own*, 9,i,1984, pp. 5–30), and in the Introduction to *The Tattooed Woman* she lists Lawrence as one of her literary models.

11 R. Kroetsch, 'On Being an Alberta Writer', *Essays*, *Open Letter*, 5th Series, 4, Spring 1983, pp. 69–80.
12 There are a number of stories in this collection which are about women with cancer, 'The Confession Tree' being the only one where a blessing is unambiguously offered in the 'benison of blossom' on the dying woman's apple tree.
13 M. Engel, Interview in G. Gibson (ed.), *Eleven Canadian Novelists*, Toronto, Anansi, 1973, p. 113.

# 8

# Arrangements, 'Disarrangements', and 'Earnest Deceptions'[1]

## Rosalie Osmond

'If I had been younger, I would have figured out a story', says the narrator at the end of 'The Stone in the Field', the second of two tales about ancestors in Alice Munro's volume of short stories, *The Moons of Jupiter*.[2] She then proceeds to give an account of the kind of story she would have 'figured out' and to contrast it with the story she has just told – which is, of course, the story Alice Munro has just written. Thus the passage functions as a justification – almost a defence (p. 35):

> I would have insisted on Mr Black's being in love with one of my aunts and on one of them – not necessarily the one he was in love with – being in love with him . . . I would have made a horrible, plausible connection between that silence of his, and the manner of this death. Now I no longer believe that people's secrets are defined and communicable, or their feelings full-blown and easy to recognize. I don't believe so. Now, I can only say, my father's sisters scrubbed the floor with lye, they stooked the oats and milked the cows by hand . . . That was their life . . . I carry something of them around in me. But the boulder is gone, Mount Hebron is cut down for gravel, and the life buried here is one you have to think twice about regretting.

In this way the narrator states her refusal to use these stories about her family to supply meanings or explanations either for her own life or for theirs. The facts remain observable, unyielding, not necessarily even mysterious. The obscure life of Mr Black, the foreigner who lived and died in a shack at the edge of the aunts' field, remains obscure not because its secret cannot be unravelled but because its secret probably does not exist, could never be anything more than a figment of the narrator's imagination.

Looking at the changes in Alice Munro's work from the early stories to the more recent ones, the reader suspects that in this passage she is really commenting on not just this particular story but on her own development as a writer. 'If I had been *younger*, I would have figured out a story'. The success of her first volume, *Dance of the Happy Shades* (1968) was assured by the felicity of just such 'figured out' stories. Calling them 'arranged' stories is not meant as a term of disparagement. They take events and distil something from them – nothing as gross as a 'lesson' or even necessarily a 'theme' – but a changed perception, a new layer of reality. At the end of the title story the perfect piece of music played by the handicapped child is characterized as a 'communiqué from the land where the old music teacher now lives'. Something definable, able to be expressed, has come out of the experience.

Even as late as the collection *Something I've Been Meaning to Tell You* (1974), we find primarily the 'arranged story'. The tale of the two sisters Et and Char, which begins the volume and shares its title with it, is a case in point. The story begins with Et and Char in late middle age discussing the reappearance of Char's old lover, Blaikie Noble. Et, the younger, less attractive and unmarried sister has gone the previous day on a bus tour for visitors to the locality, conducted by Blaikie Noble. The high point of this tour is a haunted house where a woman reputedly slowly poisoned her husband, the son of a millionaire. In the next section we discover that Char's husband, Arthur, is suffering from a variety of minor ailments with no explicable cause. Et is worried; Char is not. We then move back in time to Et's first childhood recognition of Char's beauty, a recognition that gives a new insight into her relationship with Char. Blaikie's early career as the son of the previous owner of the hotel (a sharp contrast to his present servant status) and his boyish affair with Char, which is inadvertently discovered by Et, follow. When Blaikie runs off to marry an entertainer who has been at the hotel, Char, after the heavily ironic remark 'Wouldn't that kill you?' drinks washing blueing. The blueing does not kill her; she lives to marry Arthur, a school teacher, and to pursue an apparently uneventful, childless life until the time of Blaikie's return and her husband's illness. Et works as a dressmaker and lives nearby. One day when Et is making Arthur an eggnog she finds a bottle of rat poison in Char's cupboard next to the vanilla; she is understandably disturbed. 'He would drink anything you handed him. Naturally' (p. 20). The knowledge that it is 'like something you read about, Agatha Christie', does nothing to reassure her. Long ago the troubling knowledge of Char's beauty had made her realize 'that the qualities of legend were real, that they surfaced where and when you least expected' (p. 14).

When Blaikie goes to Toronto for a day or two, Et mischievously suggests he has run away with a woman he has met at the hotel. Char, remembering the earlier elopement, believes her and is, predictably, found dead soon after. Suicide is suspected, by Et at least, but never proven. Arthur makes a partial recovery, and eventually Et moves in to look after him, troubled only by the knowledge that there is something she means to tell him – some day.

There is a certain inevitability about the events of this story. The tale of the poisoning in the haunted house prepares us for the revelation of Char's attempt to poison Arthur; the first suicide attempt by Char when she is still in her teens means that not only Et but the reader knows the likely outcome of Blaikie's much later disappearance. The use of time shifts, which juxtapose events that are separate chronologically but connected thematically, also serves to heighten this sense of inevitability. Char's first attempt to poison herself and Et's discovery of the rat poison in Char's cupboard are two such juxtaposed events. Certain pervasive motifs, such as the act of washing, also serve to give shape to the tale. It is while Char is doing the family laundry that her beauty first presents itself to Et; it is while taking in her newly washed dress from the clothes line at night that Et discovers Char and Blaikie making love; and when Char attempts suicide for the first time it is by drinking blueing. (She threatens to swallow bleach if Et tells anyone.)

The criticism of artfulness is partially defused from within the story itself by frequent observations of the way in which life seems to imitate art. Thus Char's beauty is described as a legend that has surfaced, the poisoning episode is like Agatha Christie, and the return of Blaikie just hours after Char has died is 'like some story' – later identified as *Romeo and Juliet*. The ending maintains an ironic balance between Et's secret knowledge of Char's earlier suicide attempt as well as her own guilty part in Char's final death and the picture of domestic tranquillity she and Arthur present to the world. 'If they had been married, people would have said they were very happy' (p. 29). Life may not have a fairy tale ending – Et and Arthur are not married; the 'happily ever after' remains conditional ('People *would* have said they were very happy') and, in truth, more conditional than people know or suspect – yet it follows certain predictable patterns; signs at the beginning hold in embryo the end.

It is only the *The Beggar Maid*, a collection of connected short stories published in 1978 and, to a much greater extent in the following volume, *The Moons of Jupiter* (1982) that we note a conscious movement away from this 'arranged' story. Here also, it is the words of the characters in the stories themselves that reveal most about the writer's own changing theories of story-telling.

Wilfred, in 'Visitors', from *The Moons of Jupiter*, criticizes his brother for the way he tells the tale of a man he knew in his childhood who inexplicably walked into a swamp and was believed to live there. When the brother has finished on an inconclusive note, Wilfred says, 'Is that all? They never found out what happened?'

'No.'

His wife Mildred's criticism is even more pointed (p. 215):

If Wilfred had been telling that story, Mildred thought, it would have gone some place, there would have been some kind of ending to it. Lloyd

Sallows might reappear stark naked to collect a bet, or he would come back dressed as a millionaire, maybe having tricked some gangsters who had robbed him. In Wilfred's stories you could always be sure that the gloomy parts would give way to something better, and if somebody behaved in a peculiar way there was explanation for it. If Wilfred figured a stroke of luck for him somewhere, a good meal or a bottle of whiskey or some money. Neither luck nor money played a part in this story. She wondered why Albert had told it, what it meant to him.

Albert, however, has the last word. 'It's not a story. It's something that happened' (p. 215). He seems to be asserting that reality, to him, is not patterned, meaningful. The fact that his story isn't is further proof of its authenticity.

So where is Alice Munro in this? Is Mildred the voice of the author criticizing the naive story teller who does not seem to have grasped E. M. Forster's simplest elements of plot construction? (' "The king died and then the queen died," is a story. "The king died and then the queen died of grief," is a plot.')[3] Or is it Mildred who is naive, and is Alice Munro criticizing those earlier assumptions that a tale – even a true remembered account of the past – must *go* somewhere, must have a conclusion with rewards and punishments, a clever twist, a discernible purpose underlying it all? The story from which the excerpt quoted is taken does not 'go' anywhere in Mildred's sense either. A visit between two long separated brothers and their wives reveals distances and differences that cannot be bridged. Only affection remains so that when Albert leaves, obviously a sick man, Wilfred weeps in the night that he will never see him again. Is life like this? Should stories be like this? If the modern short story is to be 'realistic', to reflect life (and the markets in which Alice Munro has been most successful are those that support this notion), then must art imitate some of the random, arbitrary and inexplicable qualities we find in life? Of course, whether we see life itself as random and arbitrary in its effects is a matter of individual perception. What I would argue is that Alice Munro increasingly does.

We can imagine this view of reality resulting in the most dreadful fiction, and, indeed, Albert's own story, isolated from its context in 'Visitors', is a case in point. Mildred has some reason to wonder why he tells it. If reality is essentially unpatterned, and the prime purpose of the story is to reflect this reality, then anyone's diary will do. The paradox is, however, that in Alice Munro's work the acceptance of the randomness of most of experience does not destroy all concept of pattern. No matter how great the insistence on the inexplicable nature of events themselves, the desire to search them for some kind of meaning, even if it is only a subjective meaning, keeps irrepressibly popping up. One aspect of this is the way Alice Munro can perceive the unexpected event as a *dis*arrangement which, in contrast to the predictably arranged story or the bare recital of events produces an initial shock and then a *re*arrangement. Thus randomness can be used not as an end in itself but as part of a quest for new, more viable patterns.

At the end of 'Simon's Luck', a chapter from *The Beggar Maid*, Rose speaks of 'those shifts of emphasis that throw the story line open to question, the *dis*-arrangements which demand new judgments and solutions, and throw the windows open on inappropriate unforgettable scenery' (p. 177). In context, it is the discovery of the death of Simon, a man with whom she has a brief but intense affair some years earlier, that strikes her as a 'disarrangement'. Thus the arbitary nature of life asserts itself against the highly artificial plots of the bland television series in which she acts, where tragic things are threatened but never happen because the audience wants to be protected from 'predictable disasters'. Simon's death gives Rose a new and startling piece of information that forces her to reassess her own attitudes. She had believed herself betrayed by him, seen herself as a victim. It now emerges that it was he who was the real victim; she is not by any means 'the only person who could seriously lack power' (p. 177). Two other stories illustrate well how Alice Munro's use of this shock of disarrangement has changed from her earlier to her later work. In both cases the 'disarrangement' in question is death or near death, but while in the earlier story the implications for the narrator are spelled out for the reader, in the latter one they are implicit. The 'disarrangement' is simply presented and left to form its own new 'arrangement' in the mind of both characters and reader alike.

'The Spanish Lady' from the collection *Something I've Been Meaning to Tell You* is the story of a woman on a train journey trying to come to terms with an unhappy marriage; her husband has now abandoned her to have an affair with her best friend. On the train trip she has an encounter with a Rosicrucian who believes in the rebirth of the soul in successive generations. This is meaning and pattern with a vengeance! He always knew, he says, 'there has to be something more in life'. He believes in 'fresh starts' (p. 181), about which the narrator is understandably sceptical. On arrival at the Vancouver train station her feelings of desperation and desertion are suddenly made articulate by the cry of an old man as he staggers and falls to the floor, dying. This 'disarrangement' focuses and puts into perspective both her marital difficulties and the Rosicrucian's optimism. On this occasion Alice Munro cannot resist making the point very explicitly (p. 184):

> By that cry Hugh, and Margaret, and the Rosicrucian, and I, everybody alive, is pushed back. What we say and feel no longer rings true, it is slightly beside the point. As if we were all wound up a long time ago and were spinning out of control, whirring, making noises, but at a touch could stop and see each other for the first time, harmless and still. This is a message; I really believe it is; but I don't see how I can deliver it.

In 'Labour Day Dinner', from *The Moons of Jupiter*, published eight years later, the emphasis on 'message' and 'delivery' has disappeared. What we have is an apparently 'unarranged' account of a holiday dinner followed by a near catastrophe that forces a certain 'rearrangement' on characters and reader alike. The mood at the dinner is one of uncertainty and discontent. Roberta feels she is being rejected by George, the man with whom she is currently trying to rebuild a new life. Her situation is tenuous, and she knows it. The two daughters from her previous marriage are poised uneasily on this Labour Day weekend between the world of their mother, where they spend the summer and that of their father, to which they must shortly return. The hostess is disturbed by her son's serious relationship with a narrowly moralistic 'Christian'. Various forms of ceremony are tried in an attempt to combat this pervasive mood of unease – the girls dress in costume, Angela plays the piano, the dinner is candlelit, the dessert an elaborate frozen concoction – but all these ploys fail. Then comes the final shock of 'disarrangement'. On the way back in the truck the family are narrowly missed by a car without lights, driven at high speed by a drunk. This time, however, what we are given is not a 'message' that must be delivered but a simple account of their response to the immediate experience (p. 159):

> They feel as strange, as flattened out and borne aloft, as unconnected with previous and future events as the ghost car was, the black fish. The shaggy branches of the pine trees are moving overhead, and under those branches the moonlight comes clear on the hesitant grass of their new lawn.

The final word belongs to one of the two girls who, in the back of the truck, are unaware of their narrow escape.

'Are you guys dead?' Eva says, rousing them: 'Aren't we home?' (p. 159). Apart from the slightly heavy irony of the first remark ('Are you guys dead?') this is an advance on the rather laboured ending of 'The Spanish Lady'. The story remains wholly descriptive detail alone. The final query, 'Aren't we home?' may be taken as pointing to arrival at a place where the unease and petty worries of the evening can be seen in perspective, or it may be read simply as the logical enquiry of anyone who wonders why the car has stopped and no one has emerged from it.

Whether explicit or implicit, then, disarrangements function as epiphanies, opening new perspectives for character and reader alike. In this way they are not opposed to 'arrangements'; they disturb the old presuppositions but lead to new arrangements. What they *are* opposed to are the too complacent arrangements that Alice Munro refers to as 'earnest deceptions'.

It is these 'earnest deceptions' that must be guarded against and purged in art as in life. The growing maturity and honesty that comes from rejecting the false comfort of these deceptions is one of the main themes of 'Dulse', also from *The Moons of Jupiter*. Lydia, the narrator, goes to a psychiatrist in order to sort out her impossible relationship with her lover, Duncan. Although Duncan has treated her badly and humiliated her, she has stuck with him for a time because he gives her a kind of security. Not only is he a 'good catch' – the kind of man every woman wants to be seen with – but his apartment and lifestyle, apparently random, have a rigidity and thought out quality that, initially, she finds attractive. It is in the psychiatrist's office, decorated in such a way as to make it even more obviously a secure haven than Duncan's apartment (blue carpet, blue and green striped upholstery) that Lydia finally rebels. 'There was a picture of boats and fishermen on the wall. Collusion somewhere, Lydia felt. Fake reassurance, provisional comfort, earnest deceptions' (p. 56).

Strangely enough, she finds herself vacationing on a small island in the Bay of Fundy where there are *real* boats and fishermen. Here she meets an elderly man who, though not a scholar, has devoted himself to the life and works of Willa Cather, who spent her summers on the island. Lydia soon discovers that he is not interested in any information about her that might disturb his uncritical admiration. 'Willa Cather lived with a woman,' Lydia said. When Mr Stanley answered he sounded flustered, and mildly upbraiding. 'They were devoted,' he said, (p. 59).

'What a lovely, durable shelter he had made for himself. He could carry it everywhere and nobody could interfere with it', Lydia comments. For the moment she rejects the attractions of the 'earnest deceptions' (she declines the offer of a too willing lover for the night, and prepares to leave for Toronto); nevertheless, their pull is real. Order and simplicity of viewpoint may be suspect because of their alliance with this kind of deception, but they are also very seductive. The tension between order and the disorder of ordinary experience that runs as a motif throughout 'Dulse' is present in both the content and style of many of these stories. In the party scene that opens 'Simon's Luck' Rose is seduced by the domesticity of her hostess – the bread, the paté, the kittens, the hanging plants. 'She wished, she often wished, that she could take such pains, that she could make ceremonies, impose herself, make bread' (p. 162). She cannot; and even her attempts are undercut by events. When she buys flowered sheets for the bed, cherries and wine for the table, her lover does not come. 'Reality' is unaccommodating. 'The mistake was in buying the wine, and the sheets and the cheese and the cherries. Preparations court disaster' (p. 166).

This dichotomy between order, which is usually allied to permanency, and disorder, which is akin to the change and flux of experience, is made even more explicit in one of the most episodic of her stories, 'Bardon Bus' (*Moons of Jupiter*). It moves between the past and present loves of the narrator and her friend, Kay, focusing on a recent idyllic affair in Australia from which the narrator is trying to recover. The ploy at the beginning is escapism – she daydreams about being an old maid in another generation, secure from the temptations of love. Other actual dreams occur within the tale, culminating in one of ethereal heavenly (and presumably eternal) embraces. Clothes that are gauzy and bright white turn out to be (p. 127):

Not just clothes but our substances, our flesh and bones and in a sense our souls. Embraces took place which started out with the usual urgency but were transformed, by the lightness and sweetness of our substance, into a rare state of content.

The vision is somewhat neutralized by her disparaging dismissal of it as 'all banality and innocence'. And recovery from her love affair, when it does come, is precipitated by the solid reality of life in an Estonian bakery where she has coffee – a Mediterranean housewife in a black dress, a child looking at the cakes, and a man talking to himself. The dream suddenly seems 'misplaced', and she concludes that there is a pleasure in rejecting romance and yielding to bare reality (p. 128):

> It's an uncalled-for pleasure in seeing how the design wouldn't fit and the structure wouldn't stand, a pleasure in taking into account all over again, everything that is contradictory and persistent and unaccommodating about life. I think so. I think there's something in us wanting to be reassured about all that, right alongside – and at war with – whatever there is that wants permanent vistas and a lot of fine talk.

The story ends, significantly, in the world of flux, with the promise of a new love affair for her friend Kay, the incorrigible optimist.

If Alice Munro sees 'reality' as essentially disordered, unpredictable, she also accepts the perennial human desire to see it as ordered, permanent, significant. How then are these contradictory elements to be acknowledged within the short story itself? The arrangements of the early work will no longer do. They cater to the desire for 'permanent vistas', but they do not square with actuality. The epiphanies of the 'disarrangements', the messages of communiqués so deeply believed in at the time, may also prove to be 'earnest deceptions'. So what course is possible?

The title short story from the most recent collection, *The Progress of Love*, seems to offer a very pessimistic solution. While the method of narration is fairly traditional, we find that 'reality' or even the simple truth about events in the past is rather difficult to uncover. Here arrangements are disrupted not by the 'disarrangements' that force a new pattern but by the undercutting of events through different versions of them. In a key episode in the story, the mother of Phemie, the narrator, burns three thousand dollars in the kitchen stove. Phemie, when she recalls this event, sees her father standing beside her mother, protecting her. She claims it was an act of love. But later, when she honestly examines her memory, she admits he was not there at all. Neither was she. And what she perceived to be an act of love, her boyfriend and her Aunt, on different occasions, call lunacy.

Furthermore, the content of the story, which contrasts Phemie's present rather free wheeling lifestyle with the religious fanaticism of her mother and grandmother, comes down pretty firmly on the side of Phemie – though, since she is also the narrator, this is hardly surprising. Commenting on her mother's life, in which every day ended with a totting up with God of her deeds and actions, Phemie observes (p. 35):

> Such a life can never be boring. And nothing can happen to you that you
> can't make use of. Even if you're racked by troubles, and sick and poor
> and ugly, you've got your soul to carry through life, like a treasure on a
> platter.

This is an extreme statement of the view of life in which everything is patterned,
significant. It may be hard, but it is not meaningless. Yet this rigid approach to
life has led Phemie's grandmother to attempt suicide when she believed her
husband to be unfaithful and has led Phemie's mother to such a violent hatred
of her father that she burns her inheritance from him, even though this means
that Phemie herself does not have the money to go to high school. Set against
this is the haphazard life of Phemie's Aunt Beryl. She eschews permanent
human ties ('I'm not used to being anybody's aunt, honey. I'm not even anybody's momma. I'm just me. Call me Beryl' (p. 40)) but is full of good nature
and generosity. Phemie, herself divorced at the time of the story, belongs more
to Beryl's world than to her mother's and the conclusion makes explicit her
evaluation of both ways of living.

She is showing a male friend 'whom she was seeing a lot of at the time'
around her old home which is up for sale. When he comments on the supposed
sexual shenanigans of the hippie commune who bought the house from her
father and decorated the walls with nudes she reacts strongly: 'Just say the words
"hippie" or "commune" and all you guys can think about is sex!' (pp. 50–1).
He assumes the room in question must have been hers as a little girl in order to
evoke such a strong reaction. And although this is not true, she says yes, it was
her room. Her justifcation is as follows (p. 58):

> It was just as well to make up. Moments of kindness and reconciliation
> are worth having, even if the parting has to come sooner or later. Phemie
> wonders if those moments aren't more valued, and deliberately gone
> after, in the setups some people like herself have now than they were in
> those old marriages, where love and grudges could be growing under-
> ground, so confused and stubborn it must have seemed they had all the
> time in the world.

Thus the fleeting relationships of the present, with their casual kindness (but a
kindness, in this case, based on deception) are contrasted with the grudges and
hatred endemic in the more permanent relationships of the past. This ending
seems to imply that provisional solutions are all one can expect in life. Order is
either an illusion or a straitjacket; arrangements and significance breed intol-
erance. The deception at the end of this story is not, of course, the same as the
'earnest deceptions' of the earlier stories; the narrator is conscious of what she
is doing and is not deceiving herself. But, like all deceptions, it can promise only
a temporary happiness.

As a work of fiction, this story is as artfully 'figured out' as any of her earlier
work. But if 'figuring out' means that the story 'goes somewhere', reinforces

our desire for pattern and significance in life, then this story rejects that as a plausible aim. Things are as they are; or perhaps they are as the narrator perceives them. Perhaps a provisional honesty is better than none at all, and happiness based on deception better than hatred.

The kinds of dichotomies Alice Munro sets up in 'The Progress of Love' lead inevitably to the somewhat pessimistic conclusion. In the last and title story of *The Moons of Jupiter* we find matters handled very differently because the premises are different. In place of the oppositions of order and randomness we find a partial accommodation of one to the other, or at least an acknowledgement that the two can exist side by side. The last illness of the narrator's father produces a tale that, on the surface, is simply a recital of events. Visits to the hospital are interspersed with an encounter with one of her two daughters, Judith, and Judith's boyfriend. The other daughter, Nichola, is incommunicado but also very much on her mind. An attempt at distraction, a shopping trip, reminds her of an earlier crisis in her life when the fear that Nichola had leukaemia precipitated a similar buying spree. Finally, a further effort at distraction, a trip to a planetarium filled with schoolchildren ('a slightly phoney temple' she calls it) produces a kind of catharsis. Presented with 'unknowns and horrible immensities' the children return to the world of the real – their canned pop and potato chips. Similarly, the narrator returns to her dying father, lightened by the experience, enabled by the fake awe of the planetarium to cope with the real awe of life and death. She can accept that her daughter Nichola is no longer her responsibility, and when she goes back to the hospital she can with equanimity both give her father a factual account of her visit to the planetarium and also explore with him the mythological significance of the names of the moons of Jupiter.

Here there is none of the deliberate patterning of an earlier story like 'Something I've Been Meaning to Tell You'. Nevertheless, through the juxtaposition of concern for her father and for her children, the fake awe of the planetarium and the real awe of the mystery of death which her father is facing, certain patterns emerge. Events do not repeat themselves as in the story of Et and Char, but situations do. Parent and child, the narrator stands in the centre of a web of relationships that recur in each generation. As for significance, it can be seen or ignored. Her father's irregular heartbeat can be an observable phenomenon charted on a hospital machine or a sign of impending death. The moons of Jupiter can be scientific discoveries or mythical luminaries. At the end of the story the narrator is faced with her own choice among these options. She 'means' to get up and go over to a tomb in the garden where she is sitting. She 'means' to look at the relief carvings, the stone pictures that go all the way around it. Then she admits, 'I always mean to look at them and I never do' (p. 233). She opts instead for the mundane comfort of coffee and something to eat before she goes back to the hospital.

Here Alice Munro has succeeded in presenting life as meaningful in human (if not in ultimate) terms, without forcing events into a pre-arranged pattern.

Order and disorder of both events and emotions co-exist. The figures on the tomb remain eternally present, but it is not mandatory to decipher them. And in the end, as in 'Bardon Bus', sustenance is found in an adherence to the concrete. No final solutions are promised, but the narrator has learned to accommodate herself to uncertainty.

The tension between these demands of order and disorder, significance and randomness remain, but they are used in a creative way. Even on the apparently random nature of the real, the creative mind must impose some order. The basic choices of narrative – where to begin, how to proceed, when to end – demand it. Perhaps true 'realism' lies not just in the passive acceptance but the active use of these oppositions in the short story. In 'The Moons of Jupiter' Alice Munro seems to have gone some way towards doing just this.

### Notes

1   This article was originally given as a paper in May 1986 and therefore does not take into account Alice Munro's work published since that date. 'The Progress of Love' was subsequently published in Britain as the title story in *The Progress of Love*, London, Chatto and Windus, 1987.
2   Editions of Alice Munro's works are those available in Britain. Original dates of publication are given in square brackets. *Dance of the Happy Shades*, Harmondsworth, Penguin, 1983 [1968]; *Something I've Been Meaning to Tell You*, Penguin, 1983 [1974]; *The Beggar Maid*, Allen Lane, 1980 (originally published in Canada in 1978 as *Who Do You Think You Are?*); *The Moons of Jupiter*, Allen Lane, 1983 [1982].
3   E. M. Forster, *Aspects of the Novel*, Harmondsworth, Penguin, 1971, p. 93.

# 9

## *The Handmaid's Tale, Cat's Eye* and *Interlunar*: Margaret Atwood's Feminist (?) Futures (?)

**Jill LeBihan**

Margaret Atwood is nothing if not formidable in her utilization of different forms in her writing. Her two latest novels are strikingly different from one another in terms of the formal traditions within which they might be placed. *Cat's Eye* (Toronto 1988) is a woman painter's cynical retrospective principally on her relationships with other women and feminism. *The Handmaid's Tale* (Toronto 1985) is most often labelled 'feminist dystopian'. I intend to call into question the use of this title here, for the way in which it has been employed to place Atwood's novel against the mainstream of fiction, conveniently reading the location and label as marginalizing. Marginalization then becomes construed as having the function of undermining the subversive effects of the text. In what follows, I will suggest some alternative readings of location, which offer the possibility of serious challenges to mainstream thought from places other than from the conventional centres of power.

Her latest collection of new poetry, *Interlunar* (Toronto 1984), contains poems whose narrators speak from locations which find echoes in the setting of *The Handmaid's Tale*.[1] They are voices that have been given to them, voices which aim to discover precisely where they have been put, voices which protest against the order which has this locational power over them. The voices in the poetry are nearly all weakened however, by disease, death, despair. *The Handmaid's Tale* is offered as a prediction of the future only if its warnings against oppressive central powers to mute protest are ignored. The world of Gilead is not quite an inevitable destiny. This kind of hope is not offered by the poetry of *Interlunar*. 'Letter From The House Of Questions' is not like the tale which has fortunately survived as proof that in some small, though ambiguous way, a protest has been registered. Instead it begins with a sense of its own inevitable annihilation:

> Everything about me is broken.
> Even my fingers, forming
> these words in the dust
> a bootprint will wipe out by morning,
> even these words.

Atwood has used a different writing genre or generic style for three of her most recent publications, then: poetry, 'feminist dystopian' novel and almost realist novel (since the bizarre or fantastic is never entirely missing from Atwood's work). I want to explore in this paper some of the connections between texts using different kinds of genre, of which Atwood makes use in her later writing: the speculative fiction and autobiographical confession of *The Handmaid's Tale*, the retrospective first person speaker of *Cat's Eye* and the less assertive narrational voices in the poetry of *Interlunar*. This study is an attempt to discover whether Atwood's work offers hope for feminist fiction in the future, whether it can challenge the positions offered to it by the literary mainstream or whether its words in the dust will be obliterated by a savage bootprint.

Putting Margaret Atwood's name on a feminist agenda immediately causes problems. In refusing to overtly align herself with the women's movement, Atwood has been seen as a reactionary artist, separating her art from her politics and undermining feminist solidarity. This latter perceived fracturing of sisterhood has been welcomed by masculist critics, who see any kind of criticism and internal political division into factions as destructive wrangling or bitching. Pro-feminist critics have also begun to reject Atwood's work as a result of her apparent distance, despite the fact that her textual concerns are very relevant to many issues discussed as 'feminist', irrespective of her personal declarations of non-alignment to specific feminist groups.[2]

The agenda of 'feminist (?) futures (?)', the reason for all the questionmarks relating to Atwood's work, converges for me at a much debated current critical problem. The questions meet at a spot marked by a 'post'. Does Atwood's writing exemplify postfeminism, postmodernism or postmodernist feminism? In what ways are these critical, political and chronological categories useful in reading her later fiction and in what ways does her writing help us better articulate these positions?

The post stands at a crossroads, as a sign pointing the (literary and critical) directions. The post marks one spot, its own stable site where it is embedded in concrete, but being a directional indicator, it is clearly attempting to order and to ease the transit of others, who look to it to learn where they are, where they have been and where they are going. Perhaps one of the biggest questions relating to the post is the one of who erects such a solid, stable, privileged signifier. For He who attaches the sign (and I use He advisedly) is the style merchant of today, the director of what is central and therefore of what is marginal. The presence of the post is a sign of the cultural times (just like fashion designer labels, it is a marker of who is in and who is out). The post is tagged to descriptions to indicate the contemporaneity of the signified. Post-modernism, Postfeminism and the like are titles which tell us the time.

But the chronological issue of the post is a vexing one, for it is a prefix which in addition to marking what is in vogue, what is current and up to date, is an attachment which also indicates time passing, and politics progressing beyond their starting points. As I read it, then, the post may seem static and upright, but in fact it is a moment of utter uncertainty. It relates at once to several planes of history, offering both a relevant connection with the movement from which it has evolved but also a distinction from those origins. The post is also generally an attachment which appears to offer some kind of engagement with current critical theory, a warning triangle – 'Caution. Theory Ahead!' – or the post can even turn out to be a sign which points the reader in a misleading direction.[3]

Elaine Risley, the narrator of *Cat's Eye*, comments upon the post problem with some bitterness. After procrastinating as far as possible, she finally enters the feminist art gallery where her retrospective collection is to be shown. She comments with irritation (p. 86):

> I don't give a glance to what's still on the walls. I hate those neo-expressionist dirty greens and putrid oranges, post this, post that. Every-thing is post these days, as if we're all just a footnote to something earlier that was real enough to have a name of its own.

Elaine Risley firmly rejects any attempt to make her a member of a post movement because she equates the post with the past. Elaine Risley distin-guishes between the past, as something which is dated and irrecoverably lost, and history, which is a subjective reconstruction influenced by elements of that past, but which is by no means the same thing. But for her the post marks not a position in an historical continuum but rather a radical break in genre, style and politics. According to the formulation of Elaine Risley here, the post becomes a sign that the past is no longer a relevant or fashionable referent. Elaine Risley wants her paintings to be current, which is why she has such ambivalent feelings about the retrospective exhibition ('first the retrospective, then the morgue' she comments). But she wants to be current on her own terms, not in post terms. 'Language is leaving me behind', she says, which is precisely what she believes the action of the post prefix to be. To have her work termed post-feminist appears to Elaine Risley to specifically date her feminism, and thereby make it outdated. This post categorization process appears to make her feminism 'past it' when she still sees it as necessary and relevant. As Margaret Atwood herself says in an introduction to *The Edible Woman*:

> The goals of the feminist movement have not been achieved and those who claim we're living in a post-feminist era are either sadly mistaken or tired of thinking about the whole subject.

*The Handmaid's Tale* confronts the issue of postfeminism in a different way from *Cat's Eye*, by having the narrator speak from a time when postfeminism is no longer meaningful because the feminist precedent has all but been eradicated in a way that Elaine Risley fears might happen as a result of it being posted. References to preceding political, historical and artistic movements are still meaningful in all these discourses in Elaine Risley's era despite her fears that dating processes are used to relegate the past rather than make reference to it. The catalogue for her exhibition, for example, describes one of the paintings as (p. 405):

A jeu d'esprit . . . which takes on the Group of Seven and reconstructs their vision of landscape in the light of contemporary experiment and post-modern pastiche.

The post prefix can no longer be attached to politics, art or history in *The Handmaid's Tale* in the way it is used in *Cat's Eye* because there is no official recognition of any preceding movements. There has been an attempt to erase awareness of a multiple and subjective past through the institution of a single, approved version of history. Gilead orthodoxy replaces various perspectives on the past which are accessible only through different histories by equating its one history with the past; this history is appointed to give access to what it propagates as the only true past which, this orthodoxy says, is to be disowned because of its corruption and dissolution. The only acceptable reality in Gilead is the present. Fantasy and memory (the personal, subjective stories confessed by the narrator) do not conform to this orthodoxy – they challenge the single historical canon which purports to tell the past as it really was. Fantasy and memory are consequently the very strategies which the narrator uses as part of her resistance of contemporaneity, erupting through the Gilead period in the regular 'Night' episodes that haunt the novel with the narrator's consciously reconstructed, or her unconscious/dream worked personal history.

Like Elaine Risley's rejection of the post label, like the unconventional narrator of the tale, the Handmaid herself, who keeps at least one of her identities secret, *The Handmaid's Tale* similarly resists labels that position it within a particular generic stream. The maintenance of a covert or multiple identity is shown in the novel to be part of a policy of subversion of the dominant, as I shall discuss later. The projection of the novel into the 22nd century, then, the intervals of fantasy and nightmare, the shifts in temporal position, the narratorial insistence that the text is just one version of a story that can be told in different ways by other people, the multiple examples of women's communities with their different (and sometimes oppositional) political struggles, the perspective given by the final chapter that what we grasp as a single text is in fact a reassembled transcription from a surviving jumble of cassette recordings: through all these strategies the novel constantly reiterates its uncertain, problematic relationship with the concept of a single reality, one identity, a truthful history as propagated by both the political orthodoxy of Gilead and by much of literary criticism today.

There are four levels of narrative time in *The Handmaid's Tale*:

1 The pre-Revolution past, characterized by the narrator's memories of her childhood with her mother, her student days with Moira, her memories of her daughter and her relationship with Luke.
2 The period of the Revolution itself, and the time immediately subsequent to that, including the time spent training at the Red Centre.
3 The main narrative time, Gileadean time. It is this narratorial period that is interrupted by the dream sequences. The Gileadean present is what the narrator is telling her tale about, although the events of this present are still retold as past occurrences, narrated retrospectively on to cassette tape, a fact of which we are informed at the final textual time level.
4 The time of the 'present' (our future?), the period of the Symposium of Gileadean Studies – 25 June 2195.

Apart from these textual times there is the question of the reader's own temporal context for the novel, her own recognition of events in the text and the placement of them within her own time scheme. For instance, some of the pre-Revolution period accounts of the novel deal with the narrator's mother's involvement in the women's movement of the late 1960s and the narrator's somewhat reactionary response to her mother's militancy. The narrator recalls witnessing the ritualistic burning of pornographic publications, for example, and she remembers the return of angry and injured women from abortion demonstrations. This is an inclusion of what can be seen as 'real history' or rather, what is sometimes called 'faction': a fictionalization or generalized account of real occurrences. This is what Linda Hutcheon calls historiographic metafiction.[4] The problem which I think this novel addresses is whether historical accounts can ever be more than 'faction'. The novel suggests that the privileging of history, notably in the form of 'authentic' first person narrative accounts of the past, as something more truthful and accurate than faction, is fallacious. The narrator insists that the tale she is telling is a 'reconstruction' which is always going to be at some level inaccurate, partial, incomplete, because it is retrospective and told by only one voice. But she suggests that this 'factitious' status, neither wholly fact nor complete fiction, is something that her story has in common with other historiographic metanarratives.

The novel operates on friction between narrative and theory, and between fiction and history. The story being told is one which comes from the personal experience of the narrating subject, although she does make use of stories told to her by others from their own lives. This first person confessional I rubs uneasily against the perspective provided by the viewing eyes of the academics which only cross the reader's field of vision at the conclusion of the novel. These organizing theoretical and editorial intrusions establish the text and 'establishmentarize' it. They drag the underground into the open, making public the story the Handmaid wanted to tell but they also attempt to uncover her secrets, trying to signpost her identity, giving her tale a stable location and thereby diffuse any resistance it might otherwise provide against the single authoritative, authentic history.

The preserved tapes on which *The Handmaid's Tale* is supposedly recorded can be viewed as vital records of the past, primary sources, a woman's voice speaking from a time when she should have been silent. The narration, because of its historical context, has become (like the scrabble game she plays) an act of subversion and rebellion. There is a level at which certain groups positioned within the women's studies category believe in these kind of recovered sources as challenges to a mainstream, canonical and patriarchal version of the past. But the narrative also consumes the past as it represents it, rewriting history by itself as its own fictional narrative, not The One Truth, but story, as the narrator insists.[5]

The narrator's story is, on one level, a subversive act, because of the time in which she lived. She lives in a dystopian time when there is a patriarchal state domination of information. To withhold information, or to spread unautho- rized material, is an act of treason for which the punishments are brutal and public. The narrator keeps a secret of her own name apart from the patronymic 'Of/fred'. Keeping this private knowledge forges a link with the past, but it is also an act of defiance, as the narrator is proving, at least to herself, that secrets can still be kept.

The private name has the same defiant linguistic pleasure for the narrator as her discovery of another piece of women's history. The carved incantation found in the bottom of her wardrobe, the pig latin joke 'Nolite te bastardes carborundorum' (don't let the bastards grind you down) is an example of women's history, literally staying in the closet. Women's history is as illicit in Gilead as homosexuality now, made subject to acts of suppression, under a similarly fearful state. The carving is a sign of the power of the secret in a time of oppression for the narrator, but the non-classically educated narrator has to ask the Commander for a translation of the coded message left by the previous Handmaid as a legacy to her follower.

The past is being reproduced at one level as a subversive act, but it is not a reproduction that is free of the determining factors of the prevailing ideology. Pig latin is a boys' school joke at the expense of classical teaching methods, but is a joke made from within the boys' school and interpretable only by the same classical scholars. Similarly, the recovery of the Handmaid's narrative by an academic institution in the 22nd century, the placing of the narrative in a literary continuum with Chaucer and all that that implies about a static canon, means that an act of feminist subversion has become part of the establishment. Elaine Risley is able to be self-conscious about this recuperation of her work since it happens in her own lifetime, and her comments are not without ambivalence (p. 15):

My career is why I'm here, on this futon, under this duvet. I'm having a retrospective, my first. The name of the gallery is Sub-Versions, one of those puns that used to delight me before they became so fashionable. I ought to be pleased by this retrospective, but my feelings are mixed; I don't like admitting I'm old enough and established enough to have such a thing, even at an alternative gallery run by a bunch of women. I find it improbable, and ominous: first the retrospective, then the morgue. But also I'm cheesed off because the Art Gallery of Ontario wouldn't do it. Their bias is toward dead foreign men.

Elaine Risley recognizes that she has become part of the feminist establishment, but she is still not taken seriously by the national art scene; that scene is still, as Atwood eloquently puts it, occupied by 'dead foreign men'.

Successful resistance for Elaine Risley depends upon standards of success set by her own culture and for Risley this means widespread, establishment recognition of her art. Risley's rebellion is public resistance to trends set both by the establishment and the 'alternatives' including mainstream feminism. For the narrator of *The Handmaid's Tale* resistance, if it is to be survived, has to remain underground. In the narrator's past, lack of public resistance was in part a result of her apathy. She writes (p. 66):

> Is that how we lived then? But we lived as usual. Everyone does, most of the time. Whatever is going on is as usual. Even this is as usual, now.
>
> We lived, as usual, by ignoring. Ignoring isn't the same as ignorance, you have to work at it . . . The newspaper stories were like dreams to us, bad dreams dreamt by others. How awful, we would say, and they were, but they were awful without being believable. They were too melodramatic, they had a dimension that was not the dimension of our lives.
>
> We were the people who were not in the papers. We lived in the blank white spaces at the edges of the print. It gave us more freedom.
>
> We lived in the gaps between the stories.

The gaps between the stories told in black print can, despite their apparent blankness be read in a number of ways. They are not necessarily invisible to the reading eye (nor to the disciplinary one). The gaps are for the narrator in her earlier, pre-Revolution life, acquiescences to 'the usual', representing ways of surviving in an oppressive patriarchal state, where it is easier to keep a low profile than to draw attention to the way in which 'the usual' is formed according to gender.

Another way of reading the white spaces is to view them as being essential to the black print, a contrast which the human eye requires before it can recognize shapes and signs to read. Christopher Dewdney explains this lucidly in his *Immaculate Perception* in a section called 'Edge Features',[6] and he also goes some way to showing here how the post can be used to illuminate and refer to the past, rather than just annihilating it (p. 38):

Our vision relies on discontinuity and change. It seems the majority of neural processing in the striate cortex consists of an analysis of edge-features. An object is perceived by its edges, the relationship of discontinuous lines. All written languages are the abstraction and distillation of only the essential edge-features necessary to perceive the form on which meaning is concomitant.

The black print never acknowledges its dependence on the white spaces with which it is discontinuous and thereby made perceptible. The consciousness has not been taught to focus on the white page against which the black letters are defined, and it is the print which is given the privileged attention as the unusual, the significant, not 'the usual' background.

The Handmaid is obliged to occupy the white space, and to live as usual. She can make this 'as usual' more than superficial by acquiescing completely, as Janine appears to do, at least initially, transforming herself into a semi-transparent blur (like 'raw egg-white', p. 139), to which no one pays attention. The narrator can, alternatively maintain only the superficial whiteness and have her own black spaces, her positive side. These do not challenge the orthodox centre page print; there is no question of their publication at that time. For the narrator in Gilead, the significances consist in the blackness of the 'Night' sequences which are as contrasts to the present white spaces in which she is supposed to invisibly subsist. By giving prominence to recollection of the subjective experience of the past, particularly as a private, illicit act, the narrator has found a way of providing Gilead with edge features.

The fantasy dream and memory of the 'Night' and the illicit relationship with Nick are the Handmaid's version of black print which has to remain invisible, whitewashed, at least while she is in Gilead. Finally, she goes the closest she can to taking over the black print and turning it to her own uses, by narrating her story in a form which clearly is intended to preserve it for others, although which others can never be known. But, of course, in this novel which is ever aware of determining power systems and the impossibility of escape from them, the controllers of the black print eventually take centre page. The mainstream academicians are the ones who transcribe, who organize, edit and publish the Handmaid's tale, and therefore relocate it firmly within the black print, once again neglecting the white ground.

I will reintroduce the post at this point. Up to now, the post has been discussed both as a signifier of chronological location – the prefix that indicates temporal movement away from origins – and it has also been discussed as the sign of the contemporary. The post has been seen, and feared (by Elaine Risley) as a marker of discontinuity and change, making the break with the past into a sign of fashion: the post as the designer label. In *The Handmaid's Tale* the character of Aunt Lydia is said to have a fondness for the either/or; that is, she cannot see the black print and the white spaces at the same time. In tune with Gilead orthodoxy, she would see the presence of the past as a threat to current stability, except that her either/or mentality enables her to deny that any vestige or reconstruction of a past remains. For Aunt Lydia there is only now.

The either/or viewpoint can be shown to be a fallacious one. The fusion of meanings into the word 'faction' shows that simple either/or divisions fail to operate at any linguistic or political level. *The Handmaid's Tale* itself proves the existence of a blend of what is considered historical fact and what is thought to be science fiction. The division of kinds of feminists into different political groups in the novel offers the possibility of feminist political, as well as literary, factions which are neither destructive bitchy squabbles nor pluralist utopias. I want to suggest that Dewdney's term 'edge-feature' is appropriate to the post because it functions as a marker of discontinuity and change, but one which illuminates the interdependence of the either/or, rather than insisting on the mutual exclusion of one term by the other.

A poem from *Interlunar* which recalls the quality of horror in some of the sequences from *The Handmaid's Tale* is 'No Name', and it comments upon a moment of stasis between dream and reality, between life and death, a transition point where there is no firm post to cling to. The scene described in the poem is in a nightmare setting, a moment where the relationship and power between the man and the narrator, against whose door he is bleeding, is not established and is entirely uncertain:

> He is a man in the act of vanishing
> one way or another.
> He wants you to let him in.
> He is like the soul of a dead
> lover, come back to the surface of the earth
> because he did not have enough of it and is still hungry
> but he is far from dead. Though the hair
> lifts on your arms and cold
> air flows over your threshold
> from him, you have never
> seen anyone so alive.

This man corpse returns with a powerful grip on the narrator, with his 'Please/In any language'. The haunting of the narrator in the poem is like those moments of the narrator's past that re-occur in *The Handmaid's Tale*. They have a narrative power over her, stories which demand to be told. She prefaces certain sections of the tale with the reluctant 'I don't want to be telling this', but somehow the narrator appreciates the necessity for her history to be recorded. 'No Name' ends with the same suspended moment with which it begins, a poem of non-progression:

> Your door is either half open
> or half closed.
> It stays that way and you cannot wake.

In the poem a third position of stasis results from failing to occupy either one position, that offered by the fully open door, or another, that provided by the fully closed door. The narrator is locked into her dreamlike state apparently because she has refused the either/or. The half-open/half-closed state becomes just a third fixed term. But there is a fourth, more mutable condition where all the positions are potentially ones that can be taken, or even all occupied at once. In the poem the narrator is locked into a dream, in the novel she is locked into a nightmarish dystopic world from which dreams are sometimes an escape, sometimes a torture. In both novel and the poem there is a tangential location which is implicit, an alternative to the fixed either/or choices, but both texts arrive finally at the rigid third term. The choice ultimately appears to be between the white space, the black print, or the stasis of indecision. The option of recognition of the fourth 'edge-feature' does not appear as a possibility.

The Handmaids themselves are supposed to have, like the poem, 'no name', no stability. This is to make them interchangeable and replaceable. The stable, pre-Revolution name to which Offred attaches herself secretively is the name that the 22nd century academic researchers really require in their belief that it will give them not just another history but a fully open door to a single, retrievable past. Their attempts to discover the narrator's secret go precisely against the attempts of the Handmaid herself to preserve this one aspect of her private body and her private past in the face of the violations of freedom being perpetrated in the state of Gilead. The state of Gilead has removed the mythical private family unit and this is nowhere more obvious than in the figure of the Handmaid herself, announcing her function in her red robes. The sexual act is transformed from the containment of the nuclear family in the pre-Revolution, when two metaphorically fused to form one, into a multiple fission of the familial unit, with the Handmaid standing for the wife, but precisely positioning herself in between the wife and the Commander as a rupture in the once traditional coupling. Unfortunately, the potential of this rupture of the private unit to deconstruct the power and hierarchy of the monogamous patriarchal family is not realized. Rather, the intervening Handmaid simply reinforces the ties that bind the Commander and the wife. The Handmaid's role is subordinate to that of the privileged couple, and she is an item in the male-controlled chain of trade in women.

The biological division of power in *The Handmaid's Tale*, then, accordingly not only to gender but also fertility, is another symptom of what Aunt Lydia is fond of, the either/or. Gender ambiguity, bisexuality or plurality of sexuality are impossibilities in Gilead. The signposts are on the genitalia. The narrator is consistent in her attempt to undermine the division into the two gendered posts which keeps her attached to the powerless and subordinate half of the binary. One of the ways in which she does this is with the repeated motif: 'context is all'. The shock of the old, the specifically dated in the modern environment – for instance, the fashions in the *Vogue* magazine, the ridiculous garments retrieved for use in Jezebel's – prompts the very important recognition that versions of normality are not static. Elaine Risley, in a world whose versions of femininity are more contradictory and complex than those of Gilead, although by no means unrelated, of course, walks up to a drunk bag-lady on the street. The incident provides Elaine with a review of the language of gender and power (p. 152):

> When I get up even, I see that this person is a woman. She's lying on her back, staring straight at me. 'Lady', she says. 'Lady, Lady.' That word has been through a lot. Noble lady, Dark Lady, she's a real lady, old-lady lace, Listen lady, Hey lady watch where you're going, Ladies room, run through with lipstick and replaced with women. But still the final word of appeal. If you want something very badly you do not say Woman, Woman, you say Lady, Lady.

The sign on the door of the toilet is run through with lipstick but the writing underneath can still be seen. The substitution of 'women' for 'ladies' as acceptable terminology does not mean that 'ladies' and all its baggage of meaning is eradicated, as the bag-lady is there to indicate with her plea. As Elaine Risley says at the beginning of the novel (p. 3):

> Time is not a line but a dimension, like the dimensions of space . . . I began then to think of time as having a shape, something you could see, like a series of liquid transparencies, one laid on top of another. You don't look back along time but down through it, like water. Sometimes this comes to the surface, sometimes that, sometimes nothing. Nothing goes away.

The selective process of recovery of the past in *The Handmaid's Tale* is used as a characterization device for the narrator and it also becomes a damning indictment of the Gilead state organization. The commander is constructed as living in the past, with 'old-fashioned values', although in a less conscious way than the narrator, who actively reconstructs her past for herself as a political and personal survival tactic. The Commander takes Offred to a Disneyland version of a brothel, nicknamed Jezebel's by the women who work there. All the prostitutes have to wear sequinned, low-cut, frivolous attire that has been salvaged from the past: bunny-girl outfits, swimming costumes, frilly lingerie. The narrator recalls (p. 247):

> 'It's like walking into the past,' says the Commander. His voice sounds pleased, delighted even. 'Don't you think?'
> I try to remember if the past was exactly like this. I'm not sure, now. I know it contained these things, but somehow the mix is different. A movie about the past is not the same as the past.

Of all things the Gileadean statesmen could choose to replicate out of the past, these men choose prostitution. The sanctioned prostitution and surrogacy of the Handmaid system has its roots in the practices of many eras and cultures, but Jezebel's recreates a trade of sexual illegitimacy, a parody of sexual relations from the immediately pre-Revolution past. The narrator emphasizes the 'inauthenticity' of her mental reconstructions of the past in her stories. But the construction behind the Gilead system appears to believe in the annihilation of the Utopian 1960s permissiveness, and a replacement of the failed fabricated world from that era by a 'natural' system, the return to the 'usual' which means a system based on female subordination, with women as items in a complex scheme of ownership and reproduction.

The tale telling functions as a reassurance of the existence of the past, that things were different once. The need to juxtapose past and present is a desire for perspective, looking down through the waters of time rather than along the line as Elaine Risley sees it, reading the sign underneath the lipstick scoring. The Handmaid says (p. 153):

> What I need is perspective. The illusion of depth, created by a frame, the arrangement of shapes on a flat surface . . . Otherwise, you live in the moment. Which is not where I want to be.

The perspective is provided by the white background to counteract the black print which fixes the subject in the moment. The subject needs to be able to see the frame, to be conscious that the arrangement of shapes on a flat surface is precisely that. Therefore there is an arranging subject in addition to an arranged one. The change of perspective is provided for the reader as much by the science fiction style of the novel and its future dystopian setting as by the narrator's recounting of her past. The shift in time-scales in the novel is part of its emphasis on avoiding complacency, of avoiding the danger of accepting the present moment as usual when at another point in time its standards would have been rejected as appalling or horrific. The dystopian genre and temporal shifts are ways of drawing attention to the frame, the arrangers, and the white space and flat surfaces which make perception of the signs and shapes possible.

*The Handmaid's Tale* demonstrates the juxtaposition of past standards of normality with present 'usualness' and within this, the function of some kind of historical evidence to jog the memory into recognition of change. As the narrator reminds us: 'Nothing changes instantaneously: in a gradually heating bathtub you'd be boiled to death before you knew it' (p. 66). In the 'Night' episodes of the novel, the narrator explains how she claims space for her thoughts, and more particularly for her past as a way of judging the temperature of the water. She recalls her mother urging her out of complacency, her mother's nagging insistence on the importance of the history of the women's movement, a selective version of the past (p. 131):

> You young people don't appreciate things, she'd say. You don't know what we had to go through, just to get you where you are. Look at him, slicing up the carrots. Don't you know how many women's bodies the tanks had to roll over just to get that far?

It is the 'Night' episodes of the novel, significantly, in which these stories from the past emerge. In the daylight, under the scrutiny of the Eyes, the narrator's recollection of the past puts her at risk. 'Night' becomes a definite, positive location from which to articulate resistance to the status quo, provided by the structural organization of the novel, interspersed as it is with these sequences which challenge the narrative of the present. Of course, Atwood does not allow this imposed structural division to go without examination. There is emphasis on the necessity of drawing attention to the frame throughout the novel and the final chapter, which claims to have organized the material in the tale, reincorporates into the academy what has up to this point been seen as a disruptive narrative strategy. But this demonstrates the impossibility of a clear division between the light and dark, the mainstream and the subversive, the inoperative 'either/or', something suggested also by the title poem from *Interlunar*:

The lake, vast and dimensionless,
doubles everything, the stars,
the boulders, itself, even the darkness
that you can walk so long in
it becomes light.

The post as a chronological locator does not mean that its terms are divided off from the theories of literature that came before or that are to follow. The post does not give privilege to the prior theories either. Rather, it insists on recalling them and partially incorporating them within the present. The post does mark out the poles between which meanings shuffle, but the movement is not necessarily between only two signposts, and the movement can be back and forth: the post does not mark the entrance to a one-way street. 'The lake' is 'vast and dimensionless' as the poem says. The posts are used to mark out sections within it, making their own patterns and boundaries. Even this marking out of areas for concern does not prevent the darkness from turning into light, or the light from fading into dark. What this means for the future is uncertain, as the narrator of *The Handmaid's Tale* concludes:

Whether this is my end or a new beginning I have no way of knowing: I have given myself over into the hands of strangers, because it can't be helped.
And so I step up, into the darkness within; or else the light.

The compromise that 'can't be helped' is the relinquishing of privacy and the safe white spaces away from print, the giving of oneself into the hands of strangers through telling a story. The most recent of Elaine Risley's paintings in *Cat's Eye* is a similar recognition of the risks of constructing a central subject, a narratorial I (or 'an oversized cat's eye marble'). The adoption of another genre, another way of telling a story in Atwood's latest novel, that is the paintings put into words: these provide another perspective on the positioning of a public subject, a subject which is both an attempt to resist the mainstream but also requires recognition provided by convention in order to achieve an effect. The frames can be stretched: Elaine Risley's latest painting, 'Unified Field Theory', is 'vertical oblong, larger than the other paintings'; *The Handmaid's Tale* is dystopian fiction, but also historiographic metafiction with a confessional journal-style first person narrator. The single identifiable generic frame is stretched to include as many different writing strategies as possible within its construction. But the story once in print or paint, as both novels' narrators accept, is not under the subject's control. Elaine Risley says, whilst looking around her exhibition (p. 409):

> I walk the room, surrounded by the time I've made; which is not a place, which is only a blur, the moving edge we live in; which is fluid, which turns back on itself, like a wave. I may have thought I was preserving something from time, salvaging something; like all those painters, centuries ago, who thought they were bringing Heaven to earth, the revelation of God, the eternal stars, only to have their slabs of wood and plaster stolen, mislaid, burnt, hacked to pieces, destroyed by rot and mildew.
>
> A leaky ceiling, a match and some kerosine would finish all this off. Why does this thought present itself to me, not as a fear, but as a temptation?
>
> Because I can no longer control these paintings, or tell them what to mean. Whatever energy they have came out of me. I'm what's left over.

Elaine Risley lives to see how her work takes off without her, how it changes with each additional post attached to it, framing it, mildewing it. *The Hand-maid's Tale* survives in a form as battered as those paintings of centuries ago. *Interlunar* is a reminder to pay attention to the lighting, to the way it colours and changes shapes, the way everything can be doubled in the reflection of that vast and dimensionless lake or else obscured and submerged without trace.

### Notes

1  Although *Interlunar* is Margaret Atwood's most recent new poetry publication, her *Selected Poems II*, containing some new work, appeared in 1986 (Toronto, Oxford University Press). In this period of many publications by Margaret Atwood, as additional evidence of her ability to manage a variety of genres, a collection of short stories also appeared: *Bluebeard's Egg*, Toronto, Seal, 1984. All further references to the texts are to the English editions: *The Handmaid's Tale*, London, Virago, 1987; *Cat's Eye*, London, Bloomsbury, 1989; *Interlunar*, London, Jonathan Cape, 1988.
2  For a typical example of the way in which Atwood's often critical approach to feminism is read as entirely destructive, see Stephen Fender's review of *Cat's Eye*, entitled 'An eyeful of feminism', *The Guardian*, Friday Review, 27 January 1989.
3  For a general introduction to the problem of the post, see *The Pirate's Fiancée* by Meaghan Morris, London Verso, 1988. This includes a comprehensive bibliography

of feminist postmodernist criticism and an introduction to 'feminism, reading, postmodernism'.

4 Linda Hutcheon's two articles on theorizing postmodernism inform much of this essay. See her 'History and/as Intertext', in John Moss (ed.), *Future Indicative*, Ottawa, University of Ottawa Press, 1987, pp. 169–84 and 'Beginning to theorize postmodernism', *Textual Practice 1*, 1, 1987.
5 See Fredric Jameson's foreword to J.-F. Lyotard's *The Postmodern Condition*, Manchester, Manchester University Press, 1986. p. xii, for a fuller discussion of 'a Nietzschen thematics of history', where stories become 'a way of forgetting'.
6 Christopher Dewdney, *The Immaculate Perception*, Toronto, Anansi, 1986.

# 10

# 'The Presence of the Past': Modernism and Postmodernism in Canadian Short Fiction[1]

## Stephen Regan

### I

Since the early days of colonial rule Canadian writers have regarded the short story as a particularly flexible and resilient medium for recording their impressions of a changing landscape. The immediate need to represent the land, its people and their experiences, has not precluded a lively sense of thematic novelty, nor inhibited the experimental and stylistic vitality of the short story in Canada. Over the course of its development, Canadian short fiction has shifted restlessly between rural wilderness and urban civilization, between the stability of a community and the instability of self, and between conventional realism and postmodernist fabulation. At its most impressive Canadian short fiction embraces region and nation while allowing the imagination freedom to explore new continents and thereby establish new situations and new relationships. The defining characteristic of the Canadian short story, then, is not strictly a matter of place, but rather a matter of consciousness: social and cultural determinants of a specifically Canadian kind continue to inform the story, whether its setting is in London or Toronto, giving the work of Canadian writers immense significance in terms of ideological and linguistic difference.

Since the 1960s a new level of national consciousness combined with new publishing opportunities has led to an increased reputation for the short story both at home and abroad. Wayne Grady's Penguin anthology identifies the short story as 'Canada's healthiest and most versatile literary genre', while the editors of the Oxford anthology declare that 'Today the position of the short story in Canadian writing is unassailable'.[2] Both of these anthologies are aimed, however, at a broad, international market and are concerned to promote a particular version of Canadian literary history with its own endemic themes and preoccupations. Within Canada itself, of course, the question of 'tradition' is a much more complex and controversial issue. Regional, as much as national, perspectives are a crucial part of the debate, with anthologies like Rudy Wiebe's *Stories from Western Canada* vying for recognition alongside Geoff Hancock's *Invisible Fictions: Contemporary Stories from Quebec*.[3]

In some cases nationalist perspectives are abandoned altogether in favour of a canon of stylistic excellence. John Metcalf, for instance, has persistently argued in his many anthologies of Canadian short fiction for a greater emphasis on form and technique as the proper criteria of judgement.[4] Even so, his anthologies are invariably Canadian in their selection of writers and in that sense they never completely abrogate a nationalist perspective. A more extreme preoccupation with narrative technique is evident in George Bowering's *Fiction of Contemporary Canada*,[5] which privileges the postmodern over conventional realism and concentrates on those texts which are most patently experimental, self-reflexive and anti-mimetic. But even here there is an implicit equation between the playfulness and imaginative vitality of postmodern fiction and the dynamic resourcefulness of western Canada, an assertion that what happens on the edges is surely more interesting than what goes on in the centre.

What lies behind these competing claims and multiple perspectives is the problematic nature of 'representation', in both formal and cultural terms. In this sense discussions about 'realism' are inseparable from the broader debate about regionalism and nationalism. It is, of course, an intensely political debate. Wayne Grady claims that the Canadian short story is descended from pioneer journalism and that its most characteristic feature is 'a realism so intimate and natural that what it describes is often mistaken for real life'.[6] John Metcalf eschews such talk of 'realism' and upholds a modernist ideal based largely on European and American models: Joyce, Mansfield, Hemingway, Faulkner, Chekhov. Nevertheless, the 'new' Canadian fiction is seen to betray anxieties about representation, straddling a narrow and tenuous line between referential and self-referential modes of narrative.[7] George Bowering is avowedly 'anti-realist', but the main weakness of his anthology is that it recognizes no inter-mediate position between 'sociological realism' and postmodernist fabulation.[8] There is, undoubtedly, a postmodernist presence in Canadian short fiction, but there is also a persistent concern with forms of representation. It is precisely this tension between experimentation and representation that has proved to be most productive in terms of narrative technique. Indeed, it might well be argued that because of this self-conscious anxiety about representing the nation, both modernism and postmodernism in Canada have developed in ways that are quite distinctive and quite different from their European and American counterparts.

The relationship between modernism and postmodernism is itself a matter of intense speculation. There is a good deal of uncertainty both inside and outside

Canada whether one should be regarded as an extension or a repudiation of the other. Modernist short fiction is usually associated with intense moments of insight or revelation (the 'epiphany'), with sustained levels of symbolism, impersonal narrative, ironic detachment and ultimate inconclusiveness. Postmodernism is construed as a more extreme form of aesthetic autonomy, openly declaring its fictive status, radically disrupting the conventional features of narrative and drawing extensively on myth and fantasy. In Canada, however, the demarcation between modernist and postmodernist strategies would appear to be less marked than in Europe and America. The continuing presence of realism, however subliminal the impulse might be, enables Canadian writers to transform a sense of social and historical difference into literary and linguistic difference. The most typical characteristic of contemporary short fiction in Canada is a form that questions narrative convention yet continues to be historically and politically responsive. As in other postcolonial cultures the problematics of language and representation associated with postmodernism are inseparable from a long history of equally troubled questions about nationhood and identity. While looking at the specific and distinctive forms that modernism and postmodernism take in Canadian literature, it is important to consider related developments within the broader postcolonial context.

The construction of postmodernism as 'autonomous' has led some critics of postcolonial writing to resist the term as a defining characteristic and to interpret such Euro-American concepts as a threat of hegemonic appropriation. Helen Tiffin argues that it is vital for new literatures to 'refuse contemporary critical enclosure' and declare their 'difference' against the universalizing tendencies of modern literary theory. While postcolonial literatures clearly exemplify many of the tendencies of postmodernism in Europe and America, they are, she argues, 'energised by different theoretical assumptions and by vastly different political motivations'.[9] In a similar way, Linda Hutcheon is concerned in A Poetics of Postmodernism to make a very careful distinction between the extreme autotelic techniques of the American surfiction and the French New New Novel and that form of writing which she defines as 'historiographic metafiction' – a form which, paradoxically, is both intensely self-reflexive and yet acknowledges 'real' historical events.[10]

She reserves the term postmodernism for these works of historiographic metafiction and argues impressively against the familiar claim that postmodernism is 'ahistorical' or 'dehistoricized'. Postmodernism is regarded here as an interrogation of history; if it rejects the idea of 'representation' it does so because of a determination to explore and create 'new meanings' rather than disclose and reveal meanings that are already 'there'. The postmodernist recognition of fiction and history as human constructs and related discourses does not lead to a denial of the past, though it does 'question whether we can ever *know* that past other than through its textualized remains'.[11] Several examples of historiographic metafiction in Linda Hutcheon's book are Canadian novels which demonstrate that 'the presence of the past' and the problems of reference to that past are significant and persistent traits in postmodernist fiction.

In many ways, then, the postmodern in Canadian short fiction might be regarded as an intensification of those problems of representation which were already implicit in its modernist phase. Just as modernism in Canadian short fiction does not entirely abandon conventional realist narrative, neither does postmodernism entirely reject the preoccupations and techniques of modernism. What they have in common is an enduring concern with 'the presence of the past.' This is not to suggest that all postmodernist fiction is historiographic; some extreme varieties of experimentation are to be found in the fabulation of Leon Rooke's 'The Woman Who Talked to Horses' or the dislocated and discontinuous form of Ray Smith's 'Cape Breton is the Thought Control Centre of Canada' (both in the Oxford anthology). Many stories in George Bowering's *Fiction of Contemporary Canada* are intensely self-reflexive and show little concern with 'the presence of the past'. Bowering's own highly self-conscious artistry is evident in 'A Short Story', with subsections titled 'Setting', 'Characters', 'Point of View', 'Symbolism', 'Theme', calling attention to the processes of fiction-making.

According to Bowering, the most truly 'experimental' writer of Canadian short fiction is Matt Cohen. Cohen's work reminds us, however, that postmodernism never entirely escapes the question of history and that discussions of anti-realism as well as realism are invariably caught up with specific social and cultural determinants. While displacing conventional realism with metafictional narrative, Cohen's work often shows the risks of too extreme an insistence on aesthetic playfulness, too decisive a break with actuality. Significantly, he returns in his latest collection of short stories, *Living on Water*,[12] to a more stable preoccupation with socio-cultural issues, especially with the Jewish family history of the closing story, 'Racial Memories'.

What is most remarkable about modern Canadian short fiction is its ability to accommodate a profound scepticism about 'truth' and 'meaning' while continuing to explore distinctly Canadian issues of a cultural and historical kind. As Linda Hutcheon points out, the interrogation of history is not a new theoretical development; but if modernism challenges the idea of ultimate, verifiable truths located in the past, then postmodernism moves a step further to assert that we cannot know the past except through its textual remains:

> What the postmodern writing of both history and literature has taught us is that both history and fiction are discourses, that both constitute systems of signification by which we make sense of the past . . . In other words, the meaning and shape are not *in the events* but *in the systems* which make those past 'events' into present historical 'facts'.[13]

One of the ways in which the problematic nature of historical knowledge manifests itself in Canadian short fiction is through the function of memory. Memory is a particularly useful device in this context because it brings into the foreground a potentially unstable form of representation and thereby challenges any simple notion of realism. Memory is also the repository of a culture, a place of growing and nurturing and so it is not surprising that we find it being used in conjunction with the device of the first person narrative in which the perceiving individual is a young or adolescent person. In this way memory becomes entwined with ideas of generational conflict and inheritance, and family history or personal history is shaped against the broader canvas of the nation's historical events and movements. This kind of narrative strategy is clearly at work in Mavis Gallant's Linnet Muir stories in *Home Truths* and Margaret Laurence's Vanessa MacLeod stories in *A Bird in the House*, as well as in a good deal of Alice Munro's short fiction. There is an obvious risk, of course, that such strategies can result in a superficial treatment of history, but the collision of personal memory and past events can also lead to a powerfully sustained critique of received history. Not surprisingly, then, a good deal of Canadian short fiction is preoccupied with secrecy and silence but in relation, that is, to specific historical and cultural events.

The most significant historical events to be recalled and remembered in modern Canadian short fiction are those which are shaped by the consequences of two world wars and the intervening Depression. Clark Blaise's 'A North American Education' is a classic example of the postwar short story which, as W. H. New argues, 'effectively manipulates first-person strategies so as to probe the emotional displacements of adolescence, change, exile and marital break-down'.[14] In an episode which is altogether characteristic of the anguished interplay of truth and memory in Canadian short fiction, the narrator gazes at a photograph of himself and his father taken shortly after their departure from Canada for the United States:

> In another picture I am standing with him on a Florida beach. I am five, he is forty-two. I am already the man I was destined to be; he is still the youth he always was . . . I am in my wet transparent underpants and I've just been swimming at Daytona Beach. It is 1946, our first morning in Florida. It isn't a vacation; we've arrived to start again, in the sun. The war is over, the border is open, the old black Packard is parked behind us.[15]

Generational conflict, emotional turmoil, the loss of innocence and geographical dislocation are all played out against a specific postwar cultural ethos. John Metcalf's 'Gentle As Flowers Make the Stones'[16] also exhibits a postwar sensibility, but one which perhaps owes something to the self-lacerating worries and satirical ploys of British writers, such as Kingsley Amis, in the 1950s and 1960s. For all his determined concentration on the poetical, lyrical qualities of style, Metcalf concedes that his own acerbic outlook is shaped by specific historical circumstances:

> One writes about where one lives. I happen to live in Canada. I *have* been writing about Canada from the viewpoint of being an immigrant to this

country and I get considerable mileage out of the comic and serious contrasts between Canada and Europe. But it's all emotionally complicated. Canada is my home. Soon, I'll have lived here more than half my life. Yet, at the same time, I'm still something of a stranger. But it's *also* true that I feel even more of a stranger in England. I'm caught between two worlds. And one of them exists only in memory.

The anguished interplay of memory and history seems inescapable, and is clearly articulated here in relation to the Second World War: 'You see, the England of my childhood which I remember so richly is totally gone . . . The Second World War ended so much'.[17]

What makes the interrogation of the past an intensely political act in Canadian short fiction is that it clearly offers a challenge to traditional accounts of history. In the context of postcolonial cultures such a challenge has far reaching implications. Stephen Slemon has argued that the problem of history for writers in such cultures 'goes beyond the simple binary of either redeeming or annihilating the past'. What they must contend with is the European 'master-narrative' of history which, as Helen Tiffin agrees, will always 'seek to contain and confine post-colonial self-interpretation'.[18] Among the various challenges to inherited concepts of history is the attempted imaginative recovery of 'those aspects of culture that have been subject to historical erasure'.[19]

It is the struggle against historical erasure which motivates the title story of Timothy Findley's *Stones*,[20] with its desperate attempt to know and understand the tragic circumstances of the Dieppe landing in August 1942. In a characteristic way the story focuses upon generational conflict and the dissolution of family, while mediating effectively between prewar and postwar perspectives. The opening of the story is infused with pleasurable memories, but the Great Depression cuts into the narrator's recollections of childhood, and August 1939 sees an unparalleled convergence of private and public sentiments (p. 198):

> Our lives continued in this way until about the time I was five – in August of 1939. Everyone's life, I suppose, has its demarcation lines . . . But the end of summer 1939 is a line drawn down through the memory of everyone who was then alive. We were all about to be pitched together into a melting pot of violence from which a few of us would emerge intact and the rest of us would perish.

The narrator of 'Stones' is Ben Max, the youngest of three children, whose impressions of 1939 are re-examined in 1987. The sustained dual focus of the narrative catches the freshness and innocence of childhood perceptions as well as the bitterness and dismay of adulthood, perpetually readjusting the child's perceptions in the context of the disillusioned present. Accordingly, the narrative is structured not by any simple linear record of events but through the subtle ebb and flow of memory. The adult narrator's interventions and revelations persist in puncturing and fracturing the 'story'. Recalling the momentous occasion of his father's enlistment, Ben tells us, 'I look back now on that moment with some alarm when I realise my father was only twenty-seven years old – an age I have long survived and doubled' (pp. 199–200).

Learning about Dieppe, refashioning its history, is central to the narrative. Dieppe, for Ben, exists only as text and image, and must finally be understood in terms of personal witness. As in so many examples of Canadian short fiction, 'received' history is interrogated in the light of individual experience (p. 210):

> I had never seen Dieppe. I had seen its face in photographs, I had read all the books and heard all the stories. The battle, of which my father had been a victim, had taken place in August of 1942 – roughly six months before he was returned to us. Long since then, in my adult years, I have seen that battle, or seen its parts, through the medium of documentary film . . . I had seen all this – the photographs, the books, the films – but I had never seen the town of Dieppe itself until that day in May of 1987 when I took my father's ashes there to scatter them.

This sudden leap of thirty-five years, from one image of Dieppe to another, is in keeping with the fractured narrative of 'Stones', with its renewed attempts to speak of 'what had gone wrong with our father at Dieppe' (p. 5). It is in contending with Dieppe – the word, the place, the event – that the narrative voice emerges self-consciously, once again undercutting any simple linear design. The continuing difficulties of knowing and understanding Dieppe are evinced in the discrepancy between the empirical record of received historical detail and the fictional reconstruction of that record in personal terms. A way of registering the complex emotional associations of Dieppe is found in the symbolism of the stones which litter the Normandy coast. This symbolism holds past and present in tension: the stones are treacherous, but they are also beautiful. It defines the relationship between father and son: 'I would have loved a stone'; and it anticipates the scattering of the father's ashes over the beaches of Dieppe: 'He felt like a powdered stone – pummelled and broken'. The stones, then, are an image of the present physical reality of Dieppe, but also tokens of history, touchstones of memory: 'The red stones look as if they have been washed in blood' (pp. 218–19).

In openly declaring the fictive nature of this particular version of events – 'our story' – the narrative testifies to the difficulty of ever fully comprehending the trauma of World War Two and its consequences for modern Canadian society: 'I have told our story. But I think it best – and I like it best – to end with all of us moving there beneath the trees in the years before the war' (p. 221). The narrative holds this shadowy image in suspension, resisting formal closure, and allows it to resonate outwards, challenging any final interpretation of 'history'. This is not to suggest that Findley settles for the despairing notion that all versions of history have equal validity. As W. H. New argues, his stories are concerned with the 'absences' in official history and with 'the fictions that societies create in the name of culture and the greater desire for power'. In a

very direct and uncompromising way, Findley's work exposes what it is that
'separates and destroys people',[21] whether it be the persistent and insidious
nature of social class or the more obvious and appalling atrocities of violence
and war.


## II


The subtle relationship between narrative strategy and the flux of memory in
Findley's 'Stones' helps to explain why the short story in Canada has proven to
be such a flexible and resilient medium for registering historical and cultural
shifts. What is also remarkable about the short story in Canada is that most of
the significant developments in fictional technique have been made by women
writers. Related issues of gender and nationality continue to shape creative
writing in Canada, as Coral Ann Howells clearly demonstrates in *Private and
Fictional Words*. There is undoubtedly an intriguing similarity between 'the
search for visibility and identity so characteristic of women's fiction and the
Canadian search for a distinctive cultural self-image'.[22] The politics of gender
and the politics of colonialism are, then, part of the same historical enterprise
which Canadian fiction has consistently sought to 'represent'. It is in this
context that the short stories of Mavis Gallant exert their claim to recognition,
and it is in terms of their specific historical and cultural determinants that the
stories are most likely to be appreciated and understood. Her sharp focus on
the lives of women both in Canada and in Europe during the war years intensifies the question of what it means to be Canadian, but also reveals a continuing
anxiety about the ways in which that experience might be conveyed through the
language and techniques of fiction. A deep unease about selfhood and nationhood manifests itself in the accompanying distrust of inherited forms of realism.
A persistent concern with dispersal and displacement is rendered through the
twists and turns of dislocated narrative.

The title of Mavis Gallant's selected 'Canadian' short stories, published in
1981 as *Home Truths*,[23] is doubly ambivalent; the instability and uncertainty of
our concept of 'home' is intimately bound up with the provisionality and
indeterminacy of 'truth(s)'. The effect is to challenge and undermine the
proverbial wisdom associated with such customary clichés. The volume is
structured around three related sections: 'At Home', 'Canadians Abroad' and
'Linnet Muir', with each section exploring a variety of regional, national and
international perspectives through multiple narrative strategies. In the process
these stories break down the traditional distinctions between history and fiction
and suggest that both are discourses by which we structure our sense of social
reality; together they challenge any simple, objective or neutral recounting of
the past.

There is throughout *Home Truths* an insistent recognition that the 'culture'
of a nation is shaped by the complex and often devious processes of memory

and language as well as by the obvious and identifiable historical 'events'. The 'At Home' and 'Canadians Abroad' sections are concerned with a fictional rearrangement of choices and possibilities which is not an end in itself but part of a larger enquiry into what W.H. New calls 'political modality'; they offer a way of rethinking the past, proposing renewed perspectives and new beginnings. The final effect of these formal and structural shifts is 'to probe the attitudinal fluctuations which result in political choices, or, broadly speaking, political action'.[24]

The working out of individual behaviour in relation to the broader social forces of the war years takes its most overtly political form in the Linnet Muir stories. Here, a young woman's choices and eventual decisions are dramatized against the prevailing political hegemony, which in the Montreal of the 1930s and 1940s is British (not French) and robustly masculine. There is no obvious chronology or linearity in the arrangement of the six stories; what they do have in common, like Margaret Laurence's Vanessa MacLeod stories in *A Bird in the House*, is a consistent first person narrative and a reliance upon memory as an informing and organizing principle.

'In Youth is Pleasure' introduces us to Linnet Muir's early socialist convictions and records her bid for independence, as she leaves her mother in New York to return to Montreal, the place of her birth. Preparing to cross the border immediately raises questions of identity and nationality, since 'in those days there was almost no such thing as a "Canadian" '. Neither inheritance nor upbringing makes for a stable identity: 'I did not feel a scrap British or English, but I was not an American either. In American schools I had refused to salute the flag' (p. 220). The story is remarkable for its carefully observed and clearly articulated socialist perceptions of wartime Canada. The country, we are reminded, 'had been in Hitler's war from the very beginning, but America was still uneasily at peace' (p. 222). Linnet recalls how her expectations of the place were not fulfilled and how, instead of 'an air of calm and grit and dedication', she found 'a poorer and a curiously empty country, where the faces of the people gave nothing away' (p. 222). It is here that the political modality of the story becomes most evident, for Linnet's crossing to wartime Canada coincides with her own particular set of decisions concerning her future independence.

It is the unexpected moments of convergence between individual consciousness and public history that shape these stories into something other than empirical records of wartime Montreal, and it is in such acts of recalling and remembering that fiction is created (pp. 225–6):

> And so that June morning and the drive through empty, sunlit, wartime streets are even now like a roll of drums in the mind. My life was my own revolution – the tyrants deposed, the constitution wrenched from unwilling hands; I was, all by myself, the liberated crowd setting the palace on fire; I was the flags, the trees, the bannered windows, the flower-decked trains. The singing and the skyrockets of the 1848 I so trustingly

believed would emerge out of the war were me, no one but me; and, as in the lyrical first days of any revolution, as in the first days of any love affair, there wasn't the whisper of a voice to tell me, 'You might compromise.'

Linnet's revolution is necessarily private, because at this stage in her life her struggle to exist as a single woman surmounts her commitment to communal politics; there is no alternative feminist initiative or political space in a context where women are 'penned in like sheep' (p. 226). She makes her compromise, even while noting in her journal that her survival means working in the capitalist system.

Where fictional and historical discourses merge most interestingly and significantly in the Linnet Muir stories is in the narrator's act of looking back and trying to establish what is 'true'. As in a good deal of Canadian short fiction, the reconstruction of the past is initiated through the reconstruction of family history. In this instance Linnet's discovery that there are at least three versions of her father's death cautions her against accepting any single, verifiable 'history'. Similarly, she discovers how frequently memory and knowledge are coloured by imagination: 'Montreal, in memory, was a leafy citadel where I knew every tree. In reality I recognized nearly nothing and had to start from scratch' (p. 235). In keeping with the uncertain history it records, the ending of the story is tentative and provisional; it declares a note of certainty about one aspect of youth, and then only retrospectively, only in the moment of its ending. The title 'In Youth is Pleasure' is not so much the assertion of a truth as the recognition of the implicit disappointments and uncertainties that may well accompany the rest of one's life.

'Between Zero and One' opens with a recollection of youth, but the narrative voice is much more assertively feminist than that of the earlier Linnet Muir story (p. 238):

> When I was young I thought that men had small lives of their own creation. I could not see why, born enfranchised, without the obstacles and constraints attendant on women, they set such close limits for themselves and why, once the limits had been reached, they seemed so taken aback.

As well as being an enquiry into the curiosities of male psychology and behaviour, the story explores the broader political and cultural climate in Montreal in the early 1940s. Like all of Mavis Gallant's stories, 'Between Zero and One' is precise about the shaping effects of history: 'At that time I was nineteen and we were losing the war' (p. 238). The title points to a vague and undefined 'space of life', that uncertain area on the graph of time before our lives reach a sense of surety and assume a kind of plotting and progression. The image belongs appropriately to the male world of those statisticians, draftsmen and civil engineers who inhabit the wartime office where Linnet Muir works, and it reinforces the story's concern with limits and numbers, with the border lines of class and nationality, as well as those of gender.

Wartime conditions determine a particularly intense form of chauvinism, including resentment among employers at having to employ women when the young men are away fighting. Linnet tells us that in her place of work she felt for the first time 'that almost palpable atmosphere of sexual curiosity, sexual resentment, and sexual fear that the presence of a woman can create where she is not wanted' (p. 244). On the basis of these feminist directives, the story develops what is surely one of the most searing political commentaries on colonial rule. The edifice which houses the office for the Research and Expansion of Wartime Industry becomes a representative symbol for a whole generation of corruption and exploitation.

The image of the space between zero and one also resonates with political significance in that it represents, among other things, the uncertain future of the nation. The men who look out of the old portraits seem to be saying 'too late, too late for you'. 'It is too late', Linnet Muir adds with fierce invective, 'for anyone else to import Chinese and Irish coolie labor and wring a railway out of them' (p. 245). The Montreal that Linnet describes is a city deeply resistant to change, where French is of no professional use to anyone and where the British insist on their superiority over other cultures.

Lines of cultural division extend in all directions, and the arrival of the domineering Mrs Ireland reminds Linnet Muir that solidarity among women in the war years is by no means assured. Mrs Ireland shows complicity with the men in believing that the money paid to female employees would be better spent on war bonds and plasma, and on further supplies of tanks and Spitfires. The relationship between Linnet and Mrs Ireland is essentially one of difference: 'different ages, different women, two lines of a graph that could never cross' (p. 260). The story ends with Linnet's memory of Mrs Ireland inveighing against marriage as they both look out at a grey sky, the unwashed window pane signifying the foreclosure of vision and change. The darkening close is not concerned solely with Mrs Ireland; it has to do with 'the men, with squares and walls and limits and numbers' (p. 260) – all those things that hinder a safe and sure progress. In this sense there is no closure to the story; a series of rhetorical questions holds it in suspense as the narrator contemplates an uncertain future: 'How do you stand if you stand upon Zero? What will the passage be like between Zero and One? And what will happen at One? Yes, what will happen?' (p. 260).

'Varieties of Exile', the third of the Linnet Muir stories, is perhaps the most explicit in terms of political consciousness and perhaps the most self-conscious in terms of its own fiction-making processes. Here, the young writer who specializes in stories about people in exile encounters Frank Cairns, one of 'a species of British immigrant known as remittance men' (p. 265), usually the banished sons of the English upper class. Unusually, though, Frank appears to have socialist ideals, and his relationship with Linnet Muir is the occasion for the story's preoccupation with radical politics in the war years. Linnet, being closer to Rosa Luxemburg than Beatrice Webb, is naturally critical of Cairns's

Fabian gradualism and exposes the British Left wing paradox of campaigning for change but also believing that there might be moral and spiritual benefits to be gained from poverty. Nevertheless, Frank Cairns is a political catalyst for the cause of international socialism (pp. 272–3):

> Wherever his opinions came from, Frank Cairns was the first person ever to talk to me about the English poor. They seemed to be a race, different in kind from other English. He showed me old copies of *Picture Post* he must have saved up from the Depression. In our hot summer train, where everyone was starched and ironed and washed and fed, we considered slum doorways and the faces of women at the breaking point. They looked like Lenin's 'remnants of nations' except that there were too many of them for a remnant.

It is through Cairns, too, that Linnet learns of Keir Hardie and the Scottish Labour Party, a more positive image of the Scots than the narrow, puritanical one familiar to many Canadians. Cairns perceives the operation of class conflict and cultural division through language, telling Linnet that 'unless the English surmounted their class obsessions with speech and accent Britain would not survive in the world after the war' (pp. 274–5). Linnet forgets about Cairns until she resurrects and then destroys a manuscript about 'a man from somewhere, living elsewhere, confident that another world was entirely possible' (p. 281). Cairns's death throws a shadow over the possibility of change at the juncture of the war's ending but Linnet's memory of him simultaneously raises a question about the proprieties of fiction: 'All this business of putting life through a sieve and then discarding it was another variety of exile; I knew that even then, but it seemed quite right and perfectly natural' (p. 281). The frankness of this fictional voice, openly declaring its own procedures, commenting on the processes of memory and knowledge, and thereby conceding its own vulnerability, is strikingly reminiscent of the narrative strategies at work in Alice Munro's short fiction, and it points more generally to a persistent trait already alluded to: the ability of the Canadian short story to maintain a vigorous scepticism about the representational claims of fiction and yet continue to grapple with social and political 'realities'. Such a trait demands that the stories be read in terms of their engagement with precise historical and cultural determinants and not as a universal expression of that much loved liberal humanist catchphrase, 'the human condition'.

## III

The preceding remarks on Mavis Gallant's short fiction apply equally well to the work of Margaret Laurence in *A Bird in the House*.[25] In these stories Canadian history is once again explored by a woman speaker whose generational conflicts typify broader social and cultural shifts. Once again the processes of memory serve to destabilize the official records of the past. The result is a fiction that seeks to render the truth of events and yet concedes that all such acts must be tentative and provisional. Like Gallant, Laurence attempts to record the social impact of two world wars and the intervening Depression, but whereas *Home Truths* is largely concerned with Montreal, *A Bird in the House* is set in a fictional town in Manitoba. At one level, its preoccupation with western Canada serves to highlight the internal conflicts of a region but at another it challenges 'the political hegemony of the society at large'.[26]

Like the Linnet Muir stories, those of Vanessa MacLeod in *A Bird in the House* form a sequence with overlapping and recurring incidents. There is a degree of progression in the stories but not in any obvious chronological or linear sense. It is the evolution of consciousness which shapes the stories; the image of the bird and the memory of her father's death keep resurfacing in Vanessa's narrative without leading to any final sense of coherence or closure. Like Linnet Muir Vanessa is an adult narrator whose recollections of youth provide a subtle and often ironic dual focus; both are women writers for whom the acquisition of an independent voice is the prelude to a growing assertion of freedom within a specific set of constraints. Both narratives are shaped by acts of 'remembering', and both draw upon the conventions of realism while simultaneously expressing late modernist doubts about traditional methods of representation.

Although the eight individual stories in *A Bird in the House* do not in themselves appear 'experimental' in form, they do make use of the kind of symbolist notation usually associated with modernist short fiction. The house of the title refers at the literal level to the home of Vanessa's grandparents but works at a symbolic level as the social and economic structure of an entire culture. The bird that enters through a broken skylight is a source of panic and disturbance, registering the feelings of restriction and confinement experienced by those, like Vanessa, who are trapped within the prevailing social formation. 'To Set Our House in Order', the second story in the collection, clearly demonstrates this opposition of interests and ideas. The living room, which is 'alien territory' to Vanessa, suggests not only a genteel way of life but a deep resistance to change. Typically, she is not allowed to 'run around' this room for fear she might displace the Dresden shepherdess from the mantel. The same precise notation of cultural attributes and expectations is applied to Grandmother MacLeod who dresses in a 'quilted black satin dressing gown' and whose voice is 'distinct and ringing like the tap of a sterling teaspoon on a crystal goblet'. Appropriately, Vanessa employs the image of a trapped bird to undercut the studied poise of her grandmother; the old woman's hair is 'bound grotesquely like white-feathered wings in the snare of her coarse night-time hairnet' (pp. 39–40).

The disparity between Grandmother MacLeod's self-assured role and Vanessa's critical response is an indication that these stories are deeply concerned with different ways of seeing and perceiving and with different levels of meaning and knowledge. In the 'forgotten recesses' of the house the only things 'actually to be seen' are drab oil paintings, trunks of unfashionable clothing and old photograph albums. But, Vanessa tells us, 'the unseen presences in these secret places I knew to be those of every person, young or old, who had ever belonged to the house and had died' (p. 42). The house is both a social structure and a structure of consciousness and memory, subject to both historical change and psychological disturbance. Much of the writing takes the form of empirical realism and yet continues to exert a symbolic potential, as the following paragraph reveals (p. 43):

> We had moved in with Grandmother MacLeod when the Depression got bad and she could no longer afford a housekeeper, but the MacLeod house never seemed like home to me. Its dark red brick was grown over at the front with Virginia creeper that turned crimson in the fall, until you could hardly tell brick from leaves.

What is crucial here is Vanessa's dissenting remark that the MacLeod house 'never seemed like home to me', but equally important is the linking of her formative childhood experiences with the years of the Depression. Under the crimson Virginia creeper the brick house looks solid, almost natural, and yet its 'small tower' and 'anaemic ferns' suggest an isolated, enfeebled existence. Through the coloured windows of the house, 'the world' might be seen as a place of continuing prosperity or regarded as a threat to one's well being. The effect of the passage is to establish the house as a structure within history, with its own set of specific cultural vantage points.

That structure, as Vanessa comes to realize, is also a structure of language. Grandmother MacLeod 'can't bear slang' because it goes against her sense of propriety, but her dialogue with Vanessa also reveals that the economic order is reinforced by 'proper' speech. In response to Vanessa's point that people are 'too broke' during the Depression to bother with tea parties, her Grandmother retorts, 'If you mean hard up, why don't you say so? It's mainly a question of management, anyway. My accounts were always in good order, and so was my house.' The MacLeods' domestic economy is further reinforced by an appeal to the conservative ethics of Protestant Christianity: ' "God loves Order", Grandmother MacLeod replied with emphasis. "You remember that, Vanessa. God loves Order – he wants each one of us to set our house in order" ' (p. 46). The final justification of class and economic superiority is an assertion of family links with an ancient clan, the lairds of Morven and the constables of the Castle of Kinlochaline. Vanessa once again exercises her dissenting conscience when she tells her Grandmother that *The Clans and Tartans of Scotland* is 'a swell book' but admits in her narrative, 'This was somewhat short of the truth' (p. 46). Her sceptical response to family mottoes – '*Be then a wall of brass. Learn to suffer. Consider the end. Go carefully*' is typical of her attitude to clichés and of her determination to find an independent voice and language. The family claim to nobility and gentility proves, of course, to be spurious, and the effect of Vanessa's encounter with Grandmother MacLeod is to expose the entire ideological basis on which colonial power rests. The exposure is all the more devastating because it emerges through a child's perspective, having been carefully focused through a range of formal and stylistic devices.

There is, however, a form of discourse that promises an alternative version of events: the discourse of lies and secrets. The function of such secrets, here and elsewhere in Canadian short fiction, is to destabilize existing records of history and emphasize the discrepancies between private and public knowledge. The death of Vanessa's Uncle Roderick in the First World War and her father's determination to conceal what actually happened is a secret that, once revealed, serves to undermine the whole moral order on which the MacLeod family depends. The revelation of this death coincides with the birth of a child and leads Vanessa to thoughts of disarray as she contemplates the seemingly random events in the changing landscape around her: 'I could not really comprehend these things, but I sensed their strangeness, their disarray. I felt that whatever God might love in this world, it was certainly not order' (p. 59). The story closes appropriately with Vanessa's sense of 'not knowing'. Such inconclusiveness is not simply a narrative strategy reminiscent of modernist short fiction, so keeping open the possibility of change and development; its primary effect is to deconstruct the prevailing ideology of Vanessa's family history, entertaining the idea of disorder rather than order and accepting provisionality and indeterminacy over any final notion of the truth.

The same urgent need to know and understand the past, coupled with a sense of disappointment and frustration, is evident in 'The Loons'. The focus here is on the lives of Canada's native people, and the story's opening paragraph extends the township of Manawaka both geographically and historically by linking the arrival of the Tonnerre family with 'the year that Riel was hung and the voices of the Metis entered their long silence' (p. 114). 'The Loons' is essentially a story of cultural division; it presents the Métis as a displaced and dispossessed people who occupy a marginal site in relation to the dominant colonial culture. It is significant, in view of the book's preoccupation with discourse, with language as a vehicle of power, that the Métis should be regarded initially in terms of speech. They do not, of course, speak the 'proper' English of Grandmother MacLeod. When Piquette joins the MacLeod family on holiday at Diamond Lake, Vanessa expects to learn the secrets of the wild. Her knowledge of the Indians, however, is conditioned largely by romantic texts. In the context of such relentless mythologizing, it becomes obvious to Vanessa that, 'as an Indian, Piquette was a dead loss' (pp. 120–1). Vanessa's tendency to idealize the descendants of Big Bear and Tecumseh is severely undercut by the squalid lifestyle Piquette endures, her betrayal by 'an English fella [who] works in the stockyards in the city' (p. 124), and her tragic death by fire.

Piquette's death coincides with changes in the environment, with government intervention, and with the conversion of the wilderness to a 'flourishing resort'. Vanessa's sitting on the government pier and looking across the water becomes an emblematic image of western Canada and the attempt to understand its place in history. The ending of the story is not sentimental, as some commentators have insisted; it is far too provisional and heavily qualified to merit such a description. Its purpose is not to grant Piquette some special intuitive wisdom but rather to expose Vanessa's own inability to comprehend the truth of things, thereby rendering unstable and problematic the nature of the past and those versions of history which would confidently define it.

By breaking down the distinctions between fictional and historical discourse these stories expose the strategies by which we construct our versions of what is real. The achievement of such stories is that they strive to represent historical events while at the same time acknowledging the vulnerability and inconclusiveness of their own fictional devices. For this reason, the method is essentially realist – but not simply realist, since the narrative is repeatedly fractured and reordered. As Peter Easingwood has argued, Margaret Laurence's technique might best be described as 'revisionary realism': it draws on realist conventions while simultaneously countering the attitudes and assumptions that realism habitually relies upon:

> The compulsion to find a new standpoint from which to present western experience informs her realism, even when its limits seem most sharply restrictive, as in the particular case of the collection of stories, *A Bird in the House.*[27]

There is further evidence here that Canadian short fiction does not fit easily into neatly prescriptive models of realism, modernism and postmodernism.

## IV

Like the work of Mavis Gallant and Margaret Laurence, the stories of Alice Munro are frequently shaped by the discourse of lies and secrets, though in a more striking and challenging way these stories question their own existence and display their own structural devices. What is most unusual about the fiction of Alice Munro is that at one level it reveals a postmodernist scepticism about the capacity of language to signify intended meanings and yet at another level exerts a sympathetic concern for those who continue to search for such meanings. Along with those narrators who quest after truth are those whose lives depend on fiction – those for whom 'truth' is not simply elusive but simply too terrible to contemplate. Paradoxically, then, the fiction of Alice Munro is a means of apprehending truth, however obliquely and incompletely; in the process, the distinction between truth and fiction is blurred and sometimes obliterated. While not in any obvious sense 'postmodernist', Alice Munro's fiction does share certain tendencies with the metafictional narratives identified by Linda Hutcheon. In keeping with the Canadian fiction already discussed, her work 'acknowledges the human urge to make order, while pointing out that the orders we create are just that: human constructs, not natural or given entities'.[28]

In this way, her work continually challenges those traditional structures of meaning and knowledge, including the structures of history, by which our lives are ordered.

It would be wrong, then, to equate Alice Munro's fiction too insistently with the metafictional techniques of postmodernism; if it appears preoccupied with its own self-reflexivity, it is equally concerned with its own *historicity*. What lends her work conviction is its intense preoccupation with a particular place and a particular community. Her stories are deeply rooted in small town Canada (usually south-western Ontario) and portray the lives (usually the lives of girls and women) in the austere years of postwar society. The Canada which she most frequently depicts is a country in transition, a Canada which has not entirely abandoned its Protestant ethics, nor completely accepted or even experienced the libertarian ideals of the 1960s. The impact of two world wars resonates throughout Munro's fiction, even in its most contemporary settings.

One of Munro's earliest stories, 'Red Dress – 1946', evokes the painful stirrings of young womanhood in a way that is reminiscent of the first person narratives of Linnet Muir and Vanessa MacLeod. The red dress is emblematic of the narrator's transition into adult sexuality: 'I saw how my breasts, in their new stiff brassiere, jutted out surprisingly, with mature authority, under the childish frills of the collar'.[29] The story aligns this moment of realization with a related shift in consciousness, from the possibility of happiness to the certainty of disappointment. In a characteristic way the perspectives of mother and daughter collude and collide, but equally characteristic is the enigmatic ending with its ambiguous assertion of selfhood: 'I understood what a mysterious and oppressive obligation I had, to be happy, and how I had almost failed it, and would be likely to fail it, every time, and she would not know' (p. 160). The painstaking hesitations and qualifications, the careful adjustments of knowledge and understanding, and the subtle modulations of tense are all familiar aspects of Munro's later fiction, but so too is the very precise placing of the narrative in a particular culture and society.

The title 'Red Dress' announces a story of fairy tale dimensions, a parable of growing up, but '1946' immediately locates that story in a distinctly postwar environment. If the story concerns the uncertain future of the adolescent, it also engages with what is undoubtedly a formative year in the history of modern Canada. The forms of consciousness and subjectivity which the story explores are themselves the products of a particular culture, not unlike that of Margaret Laurence's Manawaka. It is significant, for instance, that the making of the red dress is preceded by 'a flowered organdie dress with a high Victorian neckline' and 'a Scottish plaid outfit' (p. 147). Such details remind us that the story is not simply a parable with an essential moral about youth and age but a more complex fictional reconstruction of a specific cultural inheritance.

There is a preoccupation with the plurality and indeterminacy of meaning at a very early stage in Alice Munro's career. It is a willingness to explore the limits of realism – to harbour intense doubts about the representational value of fiction and yet to persevere in the creation of something that is true to life – that makes one of Munro's earliest and best known stories, 'The Peace of Utrecht', such an impressive achievement. The story is an anguished first person meditation in which the narrator struggles desperately to come to terms with her mother's death. More an act of exorcism than confession, it attempts to strip away the layers of memory under which the truth lies buried. Accordingly, we find layers of narrative and frequent shifts of tense as the story explores new angles of vision, new possibilities of meaning. Describing her mother's red brick house in the town of Jubilee, the narrator tells us: 'There was – there *is* – a little blind window of coloured glass beside the front door. I sat staring at it with a puzzled lack of emotional recognition' (p. 197). The image testifies to the difficulties of cognition, of knowing and responding to what is right and true, or of even remembering what indubitably exists, while the puzzling change of tense blurs the distinction between fiction and fact and cautions us against any simple or comfortable notion of the reader as passive recipient of the story. This particular story both announces and conceals its own status as fiction; while striving to build a convincing narrative structure it reveals its own fragile materials.

In one sense a celebration of the memory as the repository of thoughts and feelings, the story is also a critique of falsification: 'And what fantasies we weave around the frail figures of our childselves, so that they emerge beyond recognition incorrigible and gay' (p. 193). The story is suffused with memories, but the narrator is uncompromising in her sense of exactitude and accuracy. After painfully and guiltily recalling the early years of her mother's illness and her own eventual departure from Jubilee, she confesses, 'I find the picture is still not complete' (p. 200). Once again we encounter the problematics of fiction as the narrator resists her own '*Cowardly tender nostalgia, trying to get back to a gentler truth*', while understanding exactly why she averts her gaze from reality: 'In the ordinary world it was not possible to re-create her. The picture of her face which I carried in my mind seemed too terrible, unreal' (pp. 200–1). Part one of the story ends with a significant discovery when the narrator finds tangible evidence of her own childhood existence in her mother's home: a loose-leaf notebook in which is written, in her own hand: 'The Peace of Utrecht, 1713, brought an end to the War of the Spanish Succession' (p. 201). Characteristically, the great events of history serve as a momentary perspective for the seemingly insignificant, and the story moves on to its own intensely personal preoccupation with peace and succession.

In the second part of the story another tangible reminder of the past leads to a further clarification of events when the narrator's 'entertaining old aunts' encourage her to make use of her mother's clothes (p. 206):

> They stared back at me with grave accusing Protestant faces, for I had run up against the simple unprepossessing materialism which was the rock of their lives. Things must be used; everything must be used up, saved and

mended and made into something else and used again; clothes were to be worn.

But this awkward confrontation is only a prelude to the telling of a long-awaited secret: ' *"Did you know your mother got out of the hospital?"* ' The revelation of this event ironically transforms the relationship between the narrator and her sister Maddy, whose guilt about neglecting their mother now overshadows her own. The story of succession ends symbolically with Maddy smashing a pink cut-glass bowl and inadvertently revealing her trapped and tortured consciousness, her inability to find release from social constraints.

The same discourse of lies and secrets, the same alignment of private and public history, is evident in Munro's later work, especially in the stories of *Something I've Been Meaning To Tell You*.[30] 'Winter Wind', for instance, employs a subtle metaphoric framework so that its distinctly Canadian landscape becomes an appropriate medium for the exploration and discovery of secrets. The opening paragraph of the story very deftly conveys this landscape of memory, creating an impression of actual harshness and symbolic potential. The image of the child looking through the grandmother's window to a meandering river, the untracked snow and buried fence posts very effectively introduces what is, in essence, a story about the struggle to perceive and uncover the hidden truths of an older generation, to illuminate the present through a better knowledge of the past. What hinders this process so often in Alice Munro's fiction is a cautious reticence, a technique of survival based on 'simple, natural, poverty-bred materialism . . . a superstitious kind of delicacy, which skirts even words like *happy, frightened, sad*' (p. 191). The child in 'Winter Wind' unwittingly exposes this stern Presbyterian façade when she expresses a wish to leave the secure household of her aged relatives and return in the storm to her dying mother. By acting on what she feels to be her truest impulses, she challenges the traditional authority of her elders but also unexpectedly provokes an outburst of direct and deeply felt emotion. In attempting to clarify these events, the adult narrator of the story arrives at a crucial distinction between knowledge and understanding, and it is here that fiction justifies itself – not in any momentous revelation of the truth but in subtle and delicate adjustments of meaning and significance, in a way of seeing that will not remain content with given facts.

This realization of the aims and techniques of fiction is not easily achieved, hence the profound doubts which are expressed earlier in the story when the narrative voice urgently declares its own authenticity (p. 193):

> And how is anybody to know, I think as I put this down, how am I to know what I claim to know? I have used these people, not all of them, but some of them, before. I have tricked them out and altered them and shaped them any way at all, to suit my purposes. I am not doing that now, I am being as careful as I can, but I stop and wonder, I feel compunction.

The same people 'altered' and 'shaped' *do* reappear in a another story, 'The Ottawa Valley', which forms a later episode in the narrator's painful recollection of her mother's progressive, incurable disease. It opens with the memory of a journey 'during the War' (p. 218) from Union Station, Toronto to the Ottawa valley, but moves inwardly towards a deeper understanding of the past. This time, however, fiction proves incapable of recreating its subject; the narrator eschews any pretence at creating 'a proper story' (p. 234) and confesses that she is unable to produce anything more than a series of snapshots. In contemplating their own failure to cohere, Alice Munro's stories reveal an acutely sensitive awareness of anti-mimetic theories of art and literature. Yet almost in defiance of such scepticism about language and meaning, her fictional structures aspire towards moments of revelation and insight.

Alice Munro's most recent stories in *The Moons of Jupiter* and *The Progress of Love*[31] suggest that she has continued to develop and sustain the imaginative preoccupations of her earliest fiction. In particular there has been a noticeable concern with the discrepancies between private and public versions of history and with the various forms of discourse – songs, poems, family gossip – by which we attempt to understand the past and give it meaning in the present. But the sympathetic humanism of the stories is not primarily concerned with universal issues; the moral and cultural predicament which Munro explores is inextricably bound up with the values and ideals of a particular postwar society. The consciousness of her characters is invariably shaped by their material conditions.

The title story of *The Progress of Love* is intimately concerned with the human urge and instinct to live by fictions; it repeatedly, though reluctantly, insists on its own inventive nature: 'How hard it is for me to believe that I made that up. It seems so much the truth that it is the truth' (p. 30). The story is undoubtedly one of Munro's most formidable experimental works. In a beautifully orches- trated way, it brings together her most impressive formal ploys: the subtle modulation of tense, the interplay of active and retrospective voices, the collu- sion of memory and history, the unsettling shifts in perspective and the sus- tained effects of overlapping and multi-layered narratives. The story is not simply concerned with the problematics of fiction; it has as much to do with the problematics of cultural displacement and the problematics of moral judge- ment and assessment in a period of complex social change. One of its principal effects is to undercut all previously considered truths and absolutes, hence the implicit sense of change and development in the title. It is, above all, a story of poverty and austerity in postwar Canada and it demands to be read within precise historical and cultural terms. Its moment of consciousness is the summer of 1947, and for all its sophisticated narrative strategies 'The Progress of Love' is shaped by the same set of social and economic determinants as that much earlier story, 'Red Dress – 1946'. There are points of development but also significant continuities.

V

As well as articulating the presence of the past in Canadian culture, the work of Alice Munro also signals very clearly the remarkable emphasis in recent Canadian fiction on the active participation and involvement of the reader. This concern with reader response is, in itself, a matter of historical importance, since it involves the placing of the reader as a participant in history, in the struggle for meaning. In acting as the producers of meaning and not just its passive recipients, the readers of the text become 'the actual and actualizing links between history and fiction, as well as between the past and the present'.[32]

An overtly psychological interest in reader response is evident in the work of Audrey Thomas, whose work belongs to a tradition of women's fiction which explores the private fears and phobias of mothers, wives and daughters and yet through the very act of writing seeks to appropriate male power and dominance. At the same time, in revealing the disintegrative pressures in her characters' lives, Thomas has produced a kind of fiction which is often startlingly innovative and which seeks to mirror personal crises in terms of textual fractures, split narratives and unstable signifiers. Recently she has moved disarmingly into a genre which is neither conventional realism nor pure fantasy, producing a postmodernist metafiction or fabulation which confounds even the most lurid inventions of deconstructive critical theory.

'Kill Day on the Government Wharf' (a story which appears in the Oxford anthology) is set on one of the Gulf Islands between the city of Vancouver and Vancouver Island. Against this isolated environment Thomas describes the fretful pregnancy of a young woman from the city. Ostensibly a story of sexual jealousy and rivalry, it works almost entirely through subliminal connections which betray a deep-seated psychological unrest. The disembowelling of fish on the wharf serves as a curious objectification of this condition and proves to be both sickening and thrilling. When one of the Indian fishermen arrives at her house, dripping blood over the linoleum floor, there is a moment of confrontation between primitive existence and comfortable domesticism. The encounter is potently sexual, and while in some ways comic and awkward it remains puzzling and enigmatic (p. 303):

> He held his hands out to her and she could see, along with the seeping blood, the thin white wire-like lines of a hundred former scars. Slowly she reached out and dipped two fingers in the blood, then raised them and drew them across her forehead and down across each cheek.

Such moments of revelation suggest the presence of epiphany or what Audrey Thomas prefers to call 'a new blooming': hidden correspondences between objects and ideas, between sense and spirit, lead to mysterious unfoldings of the psyche.[33] In this particular context the unnerving parallels between repressed consciousness and images of wilderness threaten to subvert the dominant notions of settlement and civilization suggested by the presence of the *Govern-*

*ment* wharf. The story illustrates a recurring concern in Canadian fiction by exploring the deeply divided response of women to their cultural inheritance.

In her latest book, *Goodbye Harold, Good Luck*, Audrey Thomas's short stories openly declare and insist upon their own status as fiction. It is a book full of signs, messages and portents of uncertain and conflicting meanings. 'The Man With Clam Eyes' (the title itself a slip of the pen) is repeatedly disrupted by parenthetical insertions and ends with a narrator discoursing upon herself as a fictional creation. Such self-reflexive strategies seem to deny the work of fiction any claim in representing reality, and yet the story unnervingly suggests the presence of a deranged self and its perilous grip on the real world.

If Audrey Thomas's stories typify what is most usually understood by 'postmodernist fabulation', then the work of Rudy Wiebe most clearly exemplifies that specific form of postmodernism that Linda Hutcheon terms 'historiographic metafiction'. Wiebe's novels are the most powerful example in Canadian literature of fictions that appear to be 'both intensely self-reflexive and yet paradoxically also lay claim to historical events and personages'.[34] Wiebe's occasional short fiction shares the preoccupation of the novels with history and fiction as related forms of discourse, but because the short stories are partly rehearsals of more ambitious and extensive projects they also provide an immediate and revealing point of access to the theoretical concerns of historical narrative.

One of the most compelling examples of historical metafiction is Wiebe's story, 'Where is the Voice Coming From?'[35] The title sets the interrogative mood of the work, at one level initiating questions about history but at another raising intense doubts about its own authority as fiction. 'Where' functions on both levels by signifying a particular place or region but also implying an angle of approach, a matter of perspective and direction. As Coral Howells has noted, there is a fascinating link in Wiebe's fiction between prairie space and textual space; images of time are transformed into images of place, so allowing for possible revisions and reinterpretations of history.[36] What makes the notion of 'voice' problematic is that the prevailing narrative voice continually questions its own vicarious existence; in a highly self-reflexive way it acts as a surrogate for Almighty Voice, the fugitive Cree Indian whose death chant resonates beyond the formal limits of the story, forbidding any final sense of closure. The task of the narrative is to admit that banished voice into its version of history, turning absence into presence and silence into speech. The difficulties of such an endeavour are immediately apparent, as the opening sentence freely testifies: 'The problem is to make the story' (p. 135).

At first inspection, the 'facts' of what happened in the vicinity of Duck Lake, Saskatchewan Territory, between October 1895 and May 1897 might appear to be incontrovertible. Almighty Voice, a young Cree Indian, was arrested for killing a steer. In escaping police custody he shot Sergeant Colin Campbell Colebrook of the North West Mounted Police. He remained on the run for one year, two hundred and twenty days, and was finally tracked down in the

Minechinass Hills with his young relatives, Dublin and Going-up-to-Sky. Two more policemen and the postmaster from Duck Lake were shot before the three Cree Indians were themselves killed. In one sense, these acts are 'too well known', but it is precisely with the processes of knowing and not knowing that the story is concerned. It is the gaps and omissions in knowledge that undermine any simple linear narrative of events. From the outset, the narrator's attempt to recreate those events is marked by hesitations and uncertainties. All the parts of the story are 'presumably' available, but it is as if the original facts 'had from somewhere received non-factual accretions' (p. 135).

To compound the story's difficulties of cognition, the philosophical props and frameworks by which we might investigate experience or seek to understand reality – the wisdom of such thinkers as Aristotle, Teilhard de Chardin and Arnold Toynbee – are seen to be fallible or deficient. Neither hearing nor seeing can entirely relate the events of the past to the present. Several pieces of evidence are available for the narrator's empirical investigation – a piece of white bone, a seven-pounder cannon, one .44 calibre 1866 model Winchester, the police guardroom, the burial places of the dead, and a series of photographs – but none of these provides immediate or easy access. The cannon, for instance, has been 'nicely lacquered' and treated with 'nationally-advertised cleaners and restorers' (p. 137). It is the picture of Almighty Voice, however, which creates 'an ultimate problem in making the story' (p. 140), since it so obviously fails to comply with 'official' descriptions of the fugitive Indian.

It is at this point in the story that any pretence at impersonal investigation is abandoned, and the narrator openly declares his implication in the construction of events: 'I am no longer *spectator* of what *has* happened or what *may* happen: I am become *element* in what is happening at this very moment' (p. 142). The narrator has, in fact, already implicated himself in the story by having previously ascribed to a police constable the imaginary speech he now repeats (p. 142):

> *hey injun you'll get*
> *hung*
> *for stealing that steer*
> *hey injun for killing that government*
> *cow you'll get three*
> *weeks on the woodpile hey injun*

What he cannot recreate in speech but only continue to imagine is the 'unending wordless cry' of Almighty Voice's death chant (p. 143):

> I say 'wordless cry' because that is the way it sounds to me. I could be more accurate if I had a reliable interpreter who would make a reliable interpretation. For I do not, of course, understand the Cree myself.

The self-ironizing interjection 'of course' and the final emphasis on 'myself' remind us of the narrator's limited, vicarious role as a non-Cree speaker but

also point to the seemingly tentative and provisional nature of all inter-
pretations of history. This raises what is perhaps the most crucial question to be
asked of historiographic metafiction: if there is no ultimate 'truth' to be discovered, are we to assume that all versions of history have equal validity? If this is
so, then how are we to give priority to one version rather than another and
what, if anything, can be learned from the past? What sort of social and cultural
change can we envisage?

In a persuasive and exemplary essay John Thieme identifies the story as 'a
metafictive examination of the problems of constructing an accurate historical
account'. He aligns the work of Rudy Wiebe with that of other postcolonial
writers who have responded to the distortions of European historiography. In
this particular instance Wiebe is clearly concerned with the fate of Canada's
native people, and Almighty Voice is recognized as the spokesman of Cree
defiance. What makes the story 'a distinctively Canadian fiction' is its emphasis
on 'the need to rewrite history from the point of view of the dispossessed,
whose voice is not recorded in the annals of the "colonial" society'.[37] As the
essay goes on to argue, Wiebe's interests give him a greater affinity with writers
from postcolonial societies than with American contemporaries such as
Barthelme and Brautigan.

What is crucially important in the Canadian short fiction discussed here is
that history is interrogated, that received notions of 'what happened' are
continually challenged, and that the struggle for meaning, however complex
and problematic, is never abandoned. All of the stories studied in detail here are
works that rethink history and try to articulate the presence of the past. In a
postcolonial culture such a task is imperative, for its ultimate concern is with
questions of power and control, with how we come to have knowledge of the
past. It is in those nations where imbalances of power have been most evident
that the struggle for the master narrative of history is most fierce and prolonged. Writers contending with an imperialist and colonialist legacy have had
to deconstruct and demystify European 'authority' before reinscribing an independent version of history. At the end of *Translations*, a play by the Northern
Irish writer Brian Friel, we are asked to entertain the idea 'that it is not the
literal past, the "facts" of history, that shape us, but images of the past
embodied in language'.[38] This observation has a particularly apposite bearing on
the criticism of Canadian modern fiction, since one of the abiding concerns of
the short story is the shaping and dissemination of historical discourse.

From its outset Canadian short fiction has shown an intense self-
consciousness about its own powers of reference and representation. It might
well be argued that the relationships between fiction and history have therefore
always been problematic. If the Canadian short story has become increasingly
wary of the mimetic impulse of realism, it has also sedulously avoided the
impulse towards aesthetic autonomy that characterized a good deal of modernist fiction in the early twentieth century. This helps to explain why postmodernism assumed a particular form in Canadian literature, and why in some

ways it was a highly appropriate and inevitable development of earlier cultural tensions. Linda Hutcheon's argument that Canadian writers have perhaps been 'primed for the paradoxes of the postmodern by their history . . . and also by their split sense of identity, both regional and national'[39] applies very forcefully to the work of such writers as Mavis Gallant, Margaret Laurence and Alice Munro. These authors are not in any obvious sense postmodern, but their fiction is certainly characterized by a problematic regard for the presence of the past and by a profoundly divided impulse between reference and self-reference. Such fiction implies that our knowledge of history is provisional and indeterminate, a realization that seems like cause for neutrality and quietism. What these fictions also reveal, however, is that where political desire is active, meanings can be contested and structures of power transformed.

## Notes

1 The author would like to thank the publishers of *Over Here*, Spring, 1988 for permission to use material, primarily in the introduction, for this essay.
2 Wayne Grady (ed.), *The Penguin Book Of Canadian Short Stories*, Harmondsworth, Penguin, 1980, p. vi. Margaret Atwood and Robert Weaver (eds), *The Oxford Book of Canadian Short Stories in English*, Toronto, Oxford, New York, Oxford University Press, 1986, p. xviii.
3 Rudy Wiebe (ed.), *Stories from Western Canada*, Toronto, Macmillan, 1972; Geoff Hancock (ed.), *Invisible Fictions: Contemporary Stories from Quebec*, Toronto, Anansi, 1987.
4 Among John Metcalf's many useful and stimulating anthologies are *Here and Now*, edited with Clark Blaise, Toronto, Oberon Press, 1977; *Sixteen by Twelve: Short Stories by Canadian Writers*, Toronto, Ryerson Press, 1970; *Making it New: Contemporary Canadian Stories*, Toronto, Methuen, 1982, and *The Macmillan Anthology 1*, edited with Leon Rooke, Toronto, Macmillan, 1988. The introduction to *Here and Now* includes the following statement: 'To base our selection on anything other than excellence – elegance of form, precision of style, mastery of effect – would be levelling, and would eventually corrupt our intention.'
5 George Bowering (ed.), *Fiction of Contemporary Canada*, Toronto, Coach House Press, 1980.
6 *The Penguin Book of Canadian Short Stories*, p. v.
7 Barry Cameron, introduction to *Making it New*, p. viii.
8 See the introductory notes to *Fiction of Contemporary Canada*, pp. 7–21.
9 Helen Tiffin, 'Post-Colonialism, Post-Modernism and the Rehabilitation of Post-Colonial History', *Journal of Commonwealth Literature*, 10:1, 1988, p. 172.
10 Linda Hutcheon, *A Poetics of Postmodernism: History, Theory, Fiction*, New York and London, Routledge, 1988, p. 5. See also her impressive application of postmodernist theory to Canadian fiction in *The Canadian Postmodern: A Study of Contemporary Fiction*, Toronto, New York, Oxford, Oxford University Press, 1988.
11 *A Poetics of Postmodernism*, p. 20.
12 Matt Cohen, *Living on Water*, Harmondsworth, Penguin, 1989.
13 *A Poetics of Postmodernism*, p. 89.

14 W.H. New, *A History of Canadian Literature*, London, Macmillan, 1989, pp. 244, 259.
15 Clark Blaise, *A North American Education*, Don Mills, General Publishing Company, 1973, p. 165.
16 John Metcalf, *Selected Stories*, Toronto, McClelland and Stewart, 1982, pp. 229–49.
17 John Metcalf, *Kicking Against the Pricks*, Guelph, Red Kite Press, 1986, p. 3.
18 Stephen Slemon, 'Post-Colonial Allegory and the Transformation of History', *Journal of Commonwealth Literature*, 23:1, 1988, p. 158. Helen Tiffin, *ibid.*, p. 173.
19 'Post-Colonial Allegory', p. 165.
20 Timothy Findley, *Stones*, Harmondsworth, Penguin, 1988. All further references are to this edition and will be be incorporated within the text.
21 *History of Canadian Literature*, pp. 291–2.
22 Coral Ann Howells, *Private and Fictional Words: Canadian Women Novelists of the 1970s and 1980s*, London and New York, Methuen, 1987, p. 2.
23 Mavis Gallant, *Home Truths: Selected Canadian Stories*, Toronto, Macmillan, 1987. All further references are to this edition and will be incorporated within the text.
24 W.H. New, *Dreams of Speech and Violence: The Art of the Short Story in Canada and New Zealand*, Toronto, Buffalo, London, University of Toronto Press, 1987, p. 92.
25 Margaret Laurence, *A Bird in the House*, London, Macmillan, 1970. All further references are to this edition and will be incorporated within the text.
26 *A History of Canadian Literature*, p. 246.
27 Peter Easingwood, Chapter 2 in this volume.
28 *A Poetics of Postmodernism*, pp. 41–2.
29 Alice Munro, *Dance of the Happy Shades and Other Stories*, Harmondsworth, Penguin, 1988, p. 152. All further references are to this edition and will be incorporated within the text.
30 Alice Munro, *Something I've Been Meaning to Tell You*, Harmondsworth, Penguin, 1985. All further references are to this edition and will be incorporated within the text.
31 Alice Munro, *The Moons of Jupiter*, Harmondsworth, Penguin, 1987 and *The Progress of Love*, London, Fontana, 1988. All further references will be to these editions and will be incorporated within the text.
32 *The Canadian Postmodern*, p. 65.
33 Audrey Thomas, *Goodbye Harold, Good Luck*, Harmondsworth, Penguin, 1987, p. xvii.
34 *A Poetics of Postmodernism*, p. 5.
35 Rudy Wiebe, *Where is the Voice Coming From?*, Toronto, McClelland and Stewart, 1974. All further references are to this edition and will be incorporated within the text.
36 Coral Ann Howells, 'Storm Glass: The Preservation and Transformation of History in *The Diviners, Obasan, My Lovely Enemy*', papers presented at a Seminar in Canadian Literature at the University of Leeds, 23–24 September 1988, p. 1.
37 John Thieme, 'Scheherazade as Historian: Rudy Wiebe's "Where is the Voice Coming From"', *Journal of Commonwealth Literature*, 17:1, 1982, pp. 175, 179.
38 Brian Friel, *Translations*, London, Faber and Faber, 1981, p. 66.
39 *The Canadian Postmodern*, p. 4.

# Biographical Sketches of Authors Discussed, with Suggestions for Further Reading

## Armando E. Jannetta

### Some useful secondary literature

Further critical material is incorporated into the bibliographical sketches.

Atwood, Margaret, *Survival: A Thematic Guide to Canadian Literature*, Toronto, Anansi, 1972.

Davey, Frank, *Reading Canadian Reading*, Winnipeg, Turnstone, 1988.

Howells, Coral Ann, *Private and Fictional Words: Canadian Female Novelists of the 1970s and 1980s*, London, New York, Methuen, 1987.

Hutcheon, Linda, *The Canadian Postmodern: A Study of Contemporary English-Canadian Fiction*, Toronto, Oxford, New York, Oxford University Press, 1988.

Moritz, Albert and Theresa, *The Oxford Illustrated Literary Guide to Canada*, Toronto, Oxford, New York, Oxford University Press, 1987.

Moss, John, (ed.) *Future Indicative: Literary Theory and Canadian Literature*, Ottawa, University of Ottawa Press, 1987.

New, W.H., *A History of Canadian Literature*, London, Macmillan, 1989.

Ondaatje, Michael, *Faber Book of Contemporary Short Stories*, London, Faber and Faber, 1991.

Toye, William, ed., *The Oxford Companion to Canadian Literature*, Toronto, Oxford, New York, Oxford University Press, 1983.

### Margaret Atwood (b. 1939)

Born in Ottawa, she grew up in Ottawa and Toronto and spent much of her early life in the northern Ontario and Quebec bush country. She started writing at the age of five. She took her BA at the University of Toronto and was a graduate student at Radcliff College, Harvard, in 1962. During the 1960s she lived in Boston, Vancouver,

Montreal, Edmonton and since 1970 she has lived mainly in Ontario while travelling extensively. She has taught English Literature and been Writer in Residence at York University and the universities of Toronto, Alabama and New York. In 1981–82 she was Chairperson of the Writers' Union of Canada. She has published six novels, three collections of short stories, two critical studies of Canadian literature, several children's books and a collection of essays. Her first book of poems, *Double Persephone*, appeared in 1961. Since then she has published eleven volumes of poetry. *The Circle Game* won the Governor-General's Award in 1966. She is editor of the *New Oxford Book of Canadian Verse in English*. Her work has been translated into fourteen languages and her numerous awards include several honorary degrees. *The Handmaid's Tale* (1985) was shortlisted for the Booker Prize and was the winner of the Governor-General's Award. Her most recent novel, *Cat's Eye*, was published in 1989. Very much involved with Amnesty International, she lives in Toronto with the writer Graeme Gibson and their daughter.

Criticism: Rigney, Barbara Hill, *Women Writers: Margaret Atwood*, London, Macmillan, 1987.

## Neil Bissoondath (b. 1955)

Born in Trinidad and a member of a gifted and literary family. His uncles on his mother's side include V.S. Naipaul and the late Shiva Naipaul. After secondary school he emigrated to Canada. He gained a BA in French at York University, Toronto. Fluent in French and Spanish, he was an instructor in language schools in Toronto from 1977–85. The success of his short story collection *Digging up the Mountains* (1985) made him embark on a full-time writing career. *A Casual Brutality* (1989) is his first novel, and a second collection of short stories, *On the Eve of Uncertain Tomorrows* (1990), has recently been published.

Criticism: Tiffin, Helen, 'Neil Bissoondath, *Digging Up the Mountains*', *The CRNLE Reviews Journal*, 1, 1987, pp. 7–12.

## Clarke Blaise (b. 1940)

Born in North Dakota to an English–Canadian mother from Manitoba and an itinerant furniture salesman from Quebec. His nomadic youth was characterized by ceaseless moves in the America South and Midwest as well as Canada. After graduation from Denison University, Ohio, in 1961 he went to Bernard Malamud's class in creative writing at Harvard. In 1963, while at the University of Iowa Writers' Workshop, he married Bharati Mukherjee, the Bengali–Canadian novelist, with whom he has two sons. 1966 Blaise emigrated to Montreal and became a Canadian citizen in 1973. He has taught at various universities in Canada (Concordia in Montreal and York in Toronto) and the USA (Wisconsin, Iowa and Skidmore College in Saratoga, New York State) and spent two sabbaticals in India. *A North American Education: A Book of Short Fiction* (1973) was his first book. *Days and Nights in Calcutta* (1977) was written together with Bharati Mukherjee. In 1979 *Lunar Attractions* was the winner of the *Books in Canada* Award for a first novel. In 1988 he was Writer in Residence at Emory University, Atlanta. Blaise teaches now at Columbia, New York.

Criticism: Lecker, R., *On the Line: Readings in the Short Fiction of Clark Blaise, John Metcalf, and Hugh Hood*, Downsview, Ontario, University of Toronto Press, 1982, pp. 17–58.

## Matt Cohen (b. 1942)

Born in Kingston, Ontario, from a Jewish background, Matt Cohen was mainly brought up in Ottawa. He has an MA in political theory with a thesis on Albert Camus from Toronto University. After a year of lecturing in the sociology of religion at McMaster University he abandoned his teaching career in 1968 to become a full-time writer. As a Writer in Residence at the University of Alberta (1975–76), the University of Western Ontario (1981–82), and as a visiting professor of creative writing at the University of Victoria (1979–80) and the University of Bologna (1984), Italy, he remained in touch with his academic life. In 1980 he spent a period in Spain collecting material for his novel *The Spanish Doctor* (1984). The setting of much of his fiction is related to his life in the Queen Charlotte Islands, in Toronto and at the farm he owns at Verona, north of Kingston. He was fiction editor for the leading Coach House Press. He has written book reviews and articles, a radio play and two television plays, two books for children, but is best known for his novels and short stories. His latest publications include the novel *Nadine* (1986) and the short story collection *Living on Water* (1988).

Criticism: 'Armies moving in the night: the fictions of Matt Cohen', in George Woodcock, *The World of Canadian Writing: Critiques and Recollections*, Vancouver Douglas & McIntyre, 1980.

## Marian Engel (b. 1933; d. February 1985)

Born in Toronto, Marian Engel spent her childhood in Ontario and took her BA in French and German at McMaster University, Ontario and her MA at McGill University, Montreal. Her thesis topic was the English–Canadian novel since 1939. In 1960 she received a Rotary Foundation Scholarship which enabled her to study French literature at Aix-en-Provence, France. After teaching briefly in Montreal and Montana she visited Belgium, Holland, Sweden, France and England in the early 1960s. In 1962 she married a Canadian in London and worked in London and in Cyprus before returning to Canada. Her twins were born in 1964 and her first novel, *No Clouds of Glory*, appeared in 1968. She was the first Chairperson of the Writers' Union of Canada (1973–74), and won the Governor-General's Award for her controversial book *Bear* in 1976. Divorced, she lived in Toronto with her children until her death from cancer. She has been posthumously awarded the Order of Canada. She wrote seven novels, two children's books and two collections of short stories, the second of which, *The Tattooed Woman*, was published posthumously in 1985.

Criticism: Irvine, Lorna, 'Colonial Metaphors: *The Honeyman Festival* and *Lunatic Villas*', in her *Sub/version* Toronto ECW 1986, pp. 149–69. See also the special issue on Marian Engel, *Room of One's Own*, 9, 2, June 1984.

### Timothy Findley (b. 1930)

Born in Toronto, Timothy Findley was educated at schools there and elsewhere in Ontario. His first career as an actor caused him to travel widely and to write, with the encouragement of Thornton Wilder in whose play *The Matchmaker* he performed in New York and London, for the theatre, radio and television. In 1962 he turned to writing as a full time career. *The Last of the Crazy People* (1967) was his first novel. His plays for television and radio include *The Journey* (1971), winner of the Armstrong Award for radio drama. Many of the award winning documentaries were produced in collaboration with William Whitehead. *The Wars* (1977), winner of a Governor-General's Award, is probably his most well-known novel. It has been translated into nine languages and was the basis of a film directed by Robin Phillips in 1982. He lives on a farm in Cannington, Ontario.

Criticism: Hulcoop, John F., '"Look! Listen! Mark my words!" Paying attention to Timothy Findley's fictions', *Canadian Literature*, 9 (Winter 1981, pp. 22–47).

### Mavis Gallant (b. 1922)

Born in Montreal to Anglo–Scottish parents she was brought up bilingually. When she was ten, her father died, precipitating her years of wandering. In 1940 she finished high school in New York. Back in Montreal she worked briefly for the National Film Board and then as a feature writer for the *Montreal Standard*. She married but was separated from her husband before 1950 when she left Canada for extensive travelling and writing in Europe. In 1944 her first two short stories were published in *Preview*. She has long been a contributor of short stories and essays to *The New Yorker* and the *New York Times Book Review*. Despite earlier achievements her acclaim in Canada is mainly due to *From the Fifteenth District* (1979) and *Home Truths* (1981), for which she received the Governor-General's Award. In 1981 she was made an Officer of the Order of Canada. She was Writer in Residence at the University of Toronto (1983–84) and has since returned to her apartment in the Montparnasse area of Paris where she had settled in 1961. Her most recent publications are *In Transit* (1988) and *Overhead in a Balloon: Stories of Paris* (1990).

Criticism: *Canadian Fiction Magazine*, Special Issue on Mavis Gallant, 28, 1978.

### Margaret Laurence (b. 1926, d. January 1987)

Of Scots–Irish descent, she was born and brought up in the small prairie town of Neepawa, Manitoba. Her first stories were published in her high school paper. In 1947 she took her BA in English at United College (now Winnipeg University) and married John Laurence, a civil engineer, with whom she had a daughter and a son. Her husband's job took them to England, to Somali in 1950, and to Ghana in 1952, where they spent five years, and where she translated a collection of Somali folktales, wrote her first novel and a book of short stories. Her first novel *This Side Jordan*, set in Ghana, was published in 1960 while she was living in Vancouver. From 1962 to 1973 after separating from her husband, she moved to England with her two children where she wrote her famous Manawaka sequence. For *The Diviners* (1974), and *A Jest of God*

(1966), which was filmed as *Rachel, Rachel,* directed by Paul Newman and starring Joanne Woodward, she received Governor-General's Awards. Apart from the five novels of the Manawaka cycle she published a collection of essays and four children's books. Her African writings include one critical study, *Long Drums and Cannons: Nigerian Dramatists and Novelists 1952–1968* (1968). She was Writer in Residence at several Canadian universities, received twelve honorary degrees, and was appointed Chancellor of Trent University, Ontario, in 1981. Margaret Laurence was actively involved in the peace movement. In 1973 she returned to Canada and lived in Lakefield, Ontario until her death.

Criticism: Woodcock, George, ed, *A Place to Stand On: Essays By and About Margaret Laurence,* Edmonton, NeWest, 1983.

## Alistair MacLeod (b. 1936)

Born in North Battleford, Saskatchewan, he grew up in a coal-mining community in Alberta. At the age of ten he moved back to the family farm in Inverness County, Cape Breton, where his ancestors from Scotland had settled in 1791. As a young man he worked in the mines and logging camps. He obtained a teacher's certificate from Nova Scotia Teacher's College in Truro, BA and BEd degrees from St Francis Xavier University, Antigonish, and his PhD from Notre Dame University (1968). He taught at the University of Indiana for three years (1966–69) before moving to the University of Windsor, Ontario, where he now teaches English and creative writing. Currently fiction editor of *The University of Windsor Review,* he also works at the Banff School of Fine Arts in their summer creative writing programme and has held the Scottish–Canadian Writer's Exchange post in Edinburgh. His reputation rests on a small body of work – short fiction and some poetry in prestigious Canadian and American journals and two collections of short stories – *The Lost Salt Gift of Blood* (1976) and *As Birds Bring Forth the Sun and Other Stories* (1986). Two of his short stories have been honoured by inclusion in *Best American Short Stories* – 'The Boat' in 1969 and 'The Lost Salt Gift of Blood' in 1975. The former has been made into an outstanding film by the National Film Board and the latter MacLeod adapted as a play that had a successful tour through maritime communities in 1982. He is married with six children.

Criticism: Davidson, Arnold E., 'As birds bring forth the story: the elusive art of Alistair MacLeod', *Canadian Literature,* 119, Winter 1988, pp. 32–42.

## Daphne Marlatt (b. 1942)

Born in Melbourne, Australia, of English parents who had been evacuated from Penang, Malaya, in advance of the Japanese occupation. She spent six postwar years in Penang before her family emigrated to Vancouver in 1951. Marlatt enrolled for English at the University of British Columbia in 1960, became an editor of *TISH* in 1963, and on graduation in 1964 went to the University of Indiana, where she completed an MA in comparative literature (1968). After a year in Napa, California (1967–68), Vancouver (1968–69) and Madison, Wisconsin (1969–70), she returned to

Vancouver, where she worked as a freelance writer and researcher. Her first widely published works were the novella 'Sea Haven' and fifteen poems in Raymond Souster's *New Wave Canada* (1966). These were followed by the experimental long poems *Frames* (1968), retelling Hans Christian Andersen's 'The Snow Queen', and *leaf leaf/s* (1969). Her books include, among others, her major work, *Steveston* (1972), *Net Work: Selected Writing* (1980), *Here and There* (1981), the voyage poems *How Hug a Stone* (1983), and *Touch to My Tongue* (1984), and the novels *Zocalo* (1977) and *AnaHistoric* (1988). Marlatt's work during the 1970s with the British Columbia archives' oral history project resulted in two strong documentary publications: *Steveston Recollected: A Japanese–Canadian History* (1975) and *Opening Door: Vancouver's East End* (1980). She was an editor of *The Capilano Review* (1973–76) and co-edited the prose magazine *Periodics* (1977–81), the Island Writing Series and *Island*.

Criticism: Ricou, Laurie, 'Phyllis Webb, Daphne Marlatt and Similitude', in *A Mazing Space: Writing Canadian, Women Writing*, edited by Shirley Neuman and Smaro Kamboureli, Edmonton, Longspoon/NeWest, 1986.


## Alice Munro (b. 1931)

Born and brought up in Wingham, Ontario, she was an undergraduate of English at the University of Western Ontario for two years. Her first story was published in the university's literary magazine in 1950, but she had already started writing in her early teens. In 1951 she married and moved to the West Coast. She lived for twenty years in Vancouver and Victoria where her three daughters were born. In the early 1970s she returned to southern Ontario, the setting of much of her fiction. She has been Writer in Residence at the University of Queensland, Australia. Her stories are usually first published in the *New Yorker*. Munro has also written a number of television scripts. She has been honoured three times with the Governor-General's Award: 1968 for her first collection of short stories *Dance of the Happy Shades*, 1978 for *Who Do You Think You Are?* (published in England and the United States under the title *The Beggar Maid*) and most recently for *The Progress of Love* (1986). She now lives in Clinton with her second husband.

Criticism: Miller, J. ed., *The Art of Alice Munro: Saying the Unsayable*, Waterloo, University of Waterloo Press, 1984.


## Michael Ondaatje (b. 1943)

Born in Ceylon, he joined his mother in England in 1954 and was educated at Dulwich College. In 1962 he moved to Canada. After taking his BA at the University of Toronto and his MA on Edwin Muir at Queen's University, Kingston, Ontario, he taught at the University of Western Ontario (1967–70) before joining the Department of English at Glendon College, York University, in 1971. He has published eight books of poetry and three novels, of which *In the Skin of a Lion* (1987) is his latest. *The Collected Works of Billy the Kid* (1970) and *There's a Trick with a Knife I'm Learning to Do: Poems 1973–1978* (1979) won Governor-General Awards. Ondaatje has published one critical study, *Leonard Cohen* (1970); made several short films, including one on the concrete poet bp Nichol called *Sons of Captain Poetry*, and another on *The Clinton Special*, about Theatre Passe Muraille's *The Farm Show*; and edited *Personal Fictions* (1977), and *The Long Poem Anthology* (1979). He has been involved with the Coach House Press for over a decade as adviser and editor. He lives in Toronto and teaches at Glendon College.

Criticism: Ferris, Ina, 'Michael Ondaatje and the turn to narrative', in John Moss, ed., *The Canadian Novel*, Vol. IV, *Present Tense* Toronto, NC Press, 1985, pp. 73–84.

## Audrey Thomas (b. 1935)

Born in Binghampton, New York, she was educated at Smith College, with a year at St Andrews University, Scotland. She moved to Canada after her marriage in 1958 and in 1963 received her MA from the University of British Columbia. She accompanied her husband to Ghana, where she lived from 1964–66. The novels *Mrs Blood* (1970) and *Blown Figures* (1974) are both set in Western Africa. While she was in Africa she sold her first short story to the *Atlantic*. Upon returning to Vancouver she published her first short collection, *The Green Bottles* (1967), in the same year as the youngest of her three daughters was born. In 1976 she lived in Greece. She has been Visiting Professor of Creative Writing at several Canadian universities and held the Scottish–Canadian Writer's Exchange post in Edinburgh for 1985–86. Now divorced, she lives on Galiano Island, BC.

Criticism: Butling, P., 'The Cretan paradox, or where the truth lies in Latakia', *Room of One's Own*, 10, 3 & 4, 1986, pp. 105–10.

## Rudy Wiebe (b. 1934)

Born in Speedwell, Saskatchewan, he was brought up on the family farm of a small Mennonite community. Four years earlier his parents had emigrated to Canada from the Soviet Union. His first language was Low German and he was raised as a Mennonite. He began writing seriously as an undergraduate at the University of Alberta (1953–56), from which he received an MA in creative writing in 1960. Wiebe studied abroad (1957–58) at the University of Tübingen, West Germany. On his return to Canada he taught at the Mennonite Brethren Bible College and edited the *Mennonite Brethren Herald*. In 1964 he was appointed Assistant Professor of English at Goshen College, Indiana. Since 1967 he has lived in Alberta and taught English at the University of Alberta, Edmonton, where he is now Professor of English. He was chairman of the Writers' Union of Canada from 1986 to 1987. He has published seven novels, three collections of short stories, and a play. He is also the editor of six anthologies of short fiction. His 1973 novel, *The Temptation of Big Bear*, received a Governor-General's Award.

Criticism: Keith, W.J., *Epic Fiction: The Art of Rudy Wiebe*, Edmonton, Alberta University Press, 1981.

# Index